Fear and the COVID-19 Pandemic

This book explores the forms of fear that are becoming more visible in liberal democracies and how they now tend to condition our existences in a way that is detrimental to our personal freedom. The author explores how the conception of human existence that now dominates in liberal societies and that places the highest value on the preservation of life at all costs plays a significant role in this regard. He explores the origin of this form of biopolitics that has emerged after the end of the Cold War and shows how it has dramatically changed our relationship with the state and also explains how this new dynamic has been favourable to the imposition of disproportional restrictions on our individual freedom. The COVID-19 pandemic has indeed shown that when the fear of dying ends up taking precedence over any other considerations, individuals and societies are led on an illiberal path that can only contribute to the gradual erosion of their liberties and to the development and acceptance of a new type of governance that justifies the imposition of liberticidal measures. This book will appeal to scholars and students of political theory and comparative democracy, civil rights advocates, and media professionals interested in questions related to liberalism and its post-Cold War evolution.

Jean-François Caron is Associate Professor in the Department of Political Science and International Relations at Nazarbayev University where he teaches Political Theory. He is also Research Fellow at the Institute of Political Science and Administration at the University of Opole.

Fear and the COVID-19 Pandemic
A Liberticidal Virus

Jean-François Caron

LONDON AND NEW YORK

First published 2024
by Routledge
4 Park Square, Milton Park, Abingdon, Oxon OX14 4RN

and by Routledge
605 Third Avenue, New York, NY 10158

Routledge is an imprint of the Taylor & Francis Group, an informa business

© 2024 Jean-François Caron

The right of Jean-François Caron to be identified as author of this work has been asserted in accordance with sections 77 and 78 of the Copyright, Designs and Patents Act 1988.

All rights reserved. No part of this book may be reprinted or reproduced or utilised in any form or by any electronic, mechanical, or other means, now known or hereafter invented, including photocopying and recording, or in any information storage or retrieval system, without permission in writing from the publishers.

Trademark notice: Product or corporate names may be trademarks or registered trademarks, and are used only for identification and explanation without intent to infringe.

British Library Cataloguing-in-Publication Data
A catalogue record for this book is available from the British Library

ISBN: 978-1-032-48149-4 (hbk)
ISBN: 978-1-032-48187-6 (pbk)
ISBN: 978-1-003-38774-9 (ebk)

DOI: 10.4324/9781003387749

Typeset in Times New Roman
by Newgen Publishing UK

Dedicated to all the Lockeans out there

Those who would give up essential liberty to purchase a little temporary safety deserve neither liberty nor safety.

–**Benjamin Franklin**

Contents

	Introduction	1
1	Fear and the Meaning of Life	18
2	The Passage from a Lockean to a Hobbesian World	47
3	State of Emergency or a New Governance Paradigm	68
4	Recapturing Freedom	90
	References	*104*
	Index	*109*

Introduction

It goes without saying that liberal democracies are the opposite of authoritarian regimes and are superior to them. This view largely depends on the idea that, in the latter, freedom is not guaranteed because decisions are arbitrary, not bound by the rule of law, and are sometimes made based on the 'Pharaoh says' principle, as Michael Walzer noted in *Exodus and Revolution* (1985). Another reason freedom is not guaranteed in authoritarian regimes is because people are punished when they do not act as expected or do not follow the ideological mantra. 'Illegitimate fear' or 'terroristic fear', that is, being sanctioned indiscriminately and at any time for any reason, is, therefore, one (though, of course, not the only one) of the main distinctive features of these regimes that is unknown in democratic regimes, where the legislative or executive branch does not amend the rules on a whim in the middle of the night nor are people imprisoned for refusing to abide by the dominant doxa. As a result, one of the main consequences of authoritarianism is people's inability to act and think as they wish, which can only lead to the development of an impoverished conception of life that is averse to any form of civic involvement, thereby leaving them highly isolated and vulnerable to being forced to act in an unwanted way. The façade of a unified people in an authoritarian regime in which everybody seems to be sharing the same commitment to their government and the same devotion to the objective the regime is pursuing is, in fact, the direct outcome of fear. This unanimity is a clear indication of the decay of individuals' ability to express their true beliefs, as a genuine democracy is conversely defined by agonism, disagreements, and debates amongst citizens.

DOI: 10.4324/9781003387749-1

2 Introduction

Fear is, in this regard, directly connected with the absence of freedom. To paraphrase F.D. Roosevelt (who was himself influenced by Henry David Thoreau), fear paralyses any effort to move forward or to innovate and take risks. To be free, individuals must be able to enjoy peace of mind and the feeling that they will not be judged or suffer consequences for their choices or actions or for expressing their opinions on specific matters. When this is not the case, conformity develops slowly but surely, reaching a point where it becomes totalitarian after it leads to the creation of a (fake) impression of unanimity that becomes so overwhelming that an increasing number of dissenting minds gradually abandon their will to challenge a situation that is only destined to become stagnant and where genuine problems, despite being obvious to anyone, remain unspoken as if they do not exist. Minds and regimes are then doomed to become sclerosed and, in a way, this describes the sad and tragic spectacle of the final years of communism in the 1980s.

For this reason, liberal democracies are thought to differ in this regard even though they also rely on the use of fear. However, the resultant coercion is, on the contrary, thought to be legitimate and used solely as a prerequisite for social peace and order rather than for controlling citizens. Indeed, if we are to realistically assess human behaviours, the fear of punishment serves an important societal purpose. Indeed, modern reflection on humans, from Machiavelli to Michel Foucault, has been profoundly anchored in the need for people to fear being punished by the state as the only way to maintain peace, order, and stability within political associations (Caron, 2019a). If men are naturally thought to always prioritise what is good for themselves even if it comes at the expense of others' rights or interests, the possibility of being able to organise social life depends on the capacity to hinder their selfishness and find ways to force them to consider their individual actions within their broader societal context as well as the interests of others. In this regard, individuals must constantly fear punishment for an action deemed detrimental to civic order and social peace. Fear must therefore be omnipresent and affect every part of our individual lives to transform us into ethical human beings. However, unlike the terroristic form of fear in authoritarian regimes that can only lead to a state of anomy and isolation, that found in democratic societies is rather believed to be salutary and essential to

Introduction 3

social life as it tends to 'civilise people' by making them virtuous with respect to one another. Similar to religious beliefs, which are also aimed at using fear as a means of controlling humans' most anti-social behaviours, fear of laws and other similar sanctions – such as professional codes of conduct – is thought to be a necessary precondition to guarantee social cooperation. It is also thought of as that which makes intersubjective trust and collaboration possible in addition to guaranteeing equitable corrective justice by sanctioning those who have not respected these rules. When people abide by the rules, it is assumed that individuals are not coerced into refraining from pursuing certain private or public actions and are rather free to do so without having to suffer any form of interference from anyone including any authority.

Because these restrictions are basic and reasonable in a free and democratic society as well as non-violent (in the sense that they are not aimed at terrorising people), they are not as oppressive as in authoritarian states. In other words, in authoritarian regimes, fear exists in its purest form because of the arbitrariness of the government's actions, which are entirely unbound by rules; this is why it paralyses life itself, since any word, behaviour, or thought deemed to be misaligned with the prevailing ideology can trigger retaliation from the state apparatus.[1] In turn, since citizens living in democratic states are fully aware of the lines that should not be crossed, political power is a predictable beast that allows them to define freely and without worry their conception of happiness insofar as it does not infringe on their co-citizens' natural rights. Should this sole fundamental distinction lead us to conclude that individuals living in democracies empirically enjoy more freedom than their counterparts living in authoritarian regimes? Not necessarily.

We must also keep in mind that sticking to this formal appraisal of fear ('legitimate/illegitimate forms of fear') only offers a partial and problematic view when it comes to analysing people's empirical capacity to enjoy their freedom in liberal societies. In fact, those who have been living, as I have, in a society defined as 'not free' (for almost eight years now to be precise) know very well that the type of fear that leads individuals to conform is not the result of people's anxiety of being arrested, tortured, deported, or executed. Although this may be true in some very extreme cases of authoritarianism, like Hitler's Germany, Stalin's Soviet Union, or Mao's China, this is more the exception rather than the rule. On the contrary, the repressive methods authoritarian regimes use rely upon a spectrum of means aimed at domesticating the human spirit and mind in ways that will make resorting to these extreme forms of violence only in rare occurrences (Moss, 2014). Indeed, more insidious, subtle, and non-violent forms of pressure can prove themselves to be highly effective at forging a spirit of social conformity, rendering resorting to more extreme and violent measures entirely unnecessary and undesirable. Indeed, since they will inevitably be publicised, unlike non-violent means, they run the risk of fuelling the opposition at home and abroad in a way that can ultimately be detrimental to the regime's legitimacy and reputation. In most cases, a simple phone call warning one about one's involvement in a so-called unregistered organisation or one's own realisation that he/she is being tailed by a more than obvious individual will usually convince people to revert to 'the right track' when they have integrated into their psyche the belief that their dissent will necessarily lead to their social exclusion or to them being deprived of their livelihood. Václav Havel understood and very clearly described this feature of twentieth-century communist regimes. On this subject, he famously wrote the following in 1975:

> [...] What are people actually afraid of? Trials? Torture? Loss of property? Deportations? Executions? Certainly not. The most brutal forms of pressure exerted by the authorities upon the public are, fortunately, past history – at least in our circumstances. Today, oppression takes more subtle and choice forms. And even if political trials do not take place today – everyone knows how the authorities manage to manipulate them – they only represent an extreme threat, while the main thrust has moved into the sphere of existential pressure. Which, of course, leaves the core of the matter largely unchanged. [...] For fear of losing his job, the schoolteacher teaches things he does not believe; fearing for his future, the pupil repeats them after him; for fear of not being allowed to continue his studies, the young man joins the Youth League and participates in whatever of its activities are necessary; [...] Fear of the consequences of refusal leads people to take part in elections, to vote for the proposed candidates and to pretend that they regard such ceremonies as genuine elections; out of fear for

their livelihood, position or prospects, they go to meetings, vote for every resolution they have to, or at least keep silent: [I]t is fear that carries them through sundry humiliating acts of self-criticism and penitence and the dishonest filling out of a mass of degrading questionnaires; fear that someone might inform against them prevents them from giving public, and often even private, expression to their true opinions. [...] Fear of being prevented from continuing their work leads many scientists and artists to give allegiance to ideas they do not in fact accept, to write things they do not agree with or know to be false, to join official organizations or to take part in work of whose value they have the lowest opinion, or to distort and mutilate their own works. In the effort to save themselves, many even report others for doing to them what they themselves have been doing to the people they report.

(1986, pp. 4–6)

When such a fear-based strategy proves itself to be efficient and individuals abandon their quest for change and their critical spirit, their domestication is completed. After abandoning any hope of reform, they simply divert their attention in what Havel called an 'inward direction', that is, their private sphere where they can forget about the 'outside world' and focus on the material aspects of their private lives. Facilitated by the destruction of social capital and constant surveillance and their fellow countrymen's denunciation of actively engaged citizens, the authoritarian state welcomes and encourages this spill over of energy into the private sphere as it eliminates any form of political resistance, which explains why contemporary political authoritarian regimes have focused on improving their people's inward way of life, namely their material lives, which is the price of ensuring their civic apathy and silent acceptance of the state of affairs.

Despite the presence of the rule of law, division of powers, and the protection of people's freedoms enshrined in the constitution, the type of fear Havel once described is very much present in democratic societies, with the result that individuals' freedom in these entities may not be far above that of people living in authoritarian regimes. This conclusion should not come as a surprise to us. Indeed, many philosophers like John Stuart Mill or Alexis de Tocqueville have lengthily discussed how society itself can have tremendous and debilitating impacts on people's exercise of freedom, just as political tyranny does. The fear of facing the consequences of opposing the dominant doxa can indeed create a situation where individuals will refrain from pursuing certain actions or from saying certain things and conform to the will of the majority. In such cases, people's compliance with ideas that are foreign to them will not result from fear of being punished by state authorities gone rogue but rather from fear of sanction by their peers who threaten them with social ostracism. Called 'social tyranny' or 'tyranny of the majority' by Mill and de Tocqueville, this reality operates independently from the political sphere and imposes on citizens a specific mode of thinking which, if not followed or criticised, will lead non-abiding individuals to isolation and to being ignored by their peers or mocked for their defiance of the prevailing opinion (Mill, 2001). As de Tocqueville put it, individuals who oppose the dominant doxa will soon experience the impacts of their dissidence. On this, he wrote:

> In America, the majority draws a formidable circle around thought. Inside those limits, the writer is free; but unhappiness awaits him if he dares to leave them. It is not that he has to fear an auto-da-fé, but he is the butt of mortifications of all kinds and of persecutions every day. A political career is closed to him: [H]e has offended the only power that has the capacity to open it up. Everything is refused to him, even glory. Before publishing his opinions, he believed he had partisans; it seems to him that he no longer has any now that he has uncovered himself to all; for those who blame him express themselves openly, and those who think like him, without having his courage keep silent and move away. He yields, he finally bends under the effort of each day and returns to silence as if he felt remorse for having spoken the truth.[2]
>
> (2000, pp. 270–271)

What is at stake here is the fear of being ignored, of becoming a nobody, a non-existent entity in the eyes of others. Such a fear exists because that type of external recognition is essential for our wellness. As Krishnamurti wisely said, we are inwardly whirlpools of misery and mischief. Our self-realisation will therefore imply holding a position in society and being recognised by others, as if a part of who we are depends entirely on those who are surrounding us. Far from being a simple luxury we can spare, recognition is rather a psychological necessity for human beings, and it is why we inherently avoid anything that will lead to social isolation (Krishnamurti, 1995, p. 5). Paradoxically, however, this quest for external respect inevitably reinforces conformity and destroys originality since the road to recognition implies being considered a respectable human being – something that can only result from adapting our actions and behaviours within the dominant doxa to prevent being ostracised by others. Without us realising it, these free choices we make are therefore largely a sham, and they follow a pre-determined canvas that leads us to become counterfeit humans who are untrue to ourselves.

Of course, if the sources of these tyrannies differ between democracies and authoritarian regimes (emerging from civil society in the former case and from the state apparatus itself in the latter), their consequences are, nonetheless, the same. Out of fear of facing the various impacts on one's life, whether it is becoming socially isolated or losing one's job (which would lead to the development of a deep sense of insecurity), these menaces act like an invisible hand that leads people themselves to choose to restrict their own freedom. From this perspective, we should not let ourselves be fooled by the common distinction between the lack or presence of a rule of law in order to assess people's capacity to exercise their freedom since fear can take other forms and lead to the same debilitating consequences on our liberty irrespective of the types of political regimes in which we are living. From this perspective, it is important to realise that individuals living in democracies are not immune from facing serious limitations on their freedom due to the anxiety these subtle threats arouse and that the limitations on their liberty can be similar to those of people living in an authoritarian regime are experiencing.[3]

Hence, democracies are imperfect at guaranteeing people's freedom despite the presence of a rule of law and a division of powers. The already well-known impacts of social tyranny are there to act as a gentle reminder of this unfortunate reality for which we are still trying to find a remedy. What is more worrying, however, is the fact that democracies have not always been impermeable to the aforementioned authoritarian means where the state (and not society) is the source of the subtle pressures Havel described. This was, for instance, notoriously the case during the period of 'McCarthyism' in the United States that saw thousands of Americans persecuted for their alleged ties with communism. With the notable exception of Ethel and Julius Rosenberg, who were executed for espionage on behalf of the Union of Soviet Socialist Republics, and the few dozens of leaders and members of the Communist Party who were arrested and convicted, no other individuals who got caught in the infernal machine of the 'Red Scare' were victims of physical violence. The real pressure came from the infamous Senate Permanent Subcommittee on Investigations led by Senator Joseph McCarthy that held public hearings involving individuals and publicly announced the names of persons who were thought (with reason or not) to have had ties with communism. This public humiliation that resembled Stalin's 1930s Moscow trials ultimately led many individuals working in the entertainment business to be blacklisted for their 'un-American feelings' and prevented from working. This had a snowball effect on private entities, with some of them also establishing loyalty review boards tasked with screening employees' dedication to the American way of life.

If this episode is thought to be an unfortunate exception to what democracies ought to be about, we must also recognise that the recent coronavirus disease (COVID-19) pandemic has also shown that the potential of democracies acting in a way that is surprisingly similar to the behaviour of authoritarian states by having the state apparatus apply subtle pressure is still very much a possibility that has not disappeared with the demise of Joseph McCarthy. For instance, although no liberal democracies imposed mandatory vaccination[4] for citizens, the fact is that refusing vaccination came at a tremendous price for those who opted out. Terminating the employment contracts of the unvaccinated or denying them entry to places where the status of being vaccinated was a prerequisite for access (this included, in some cases, universities)[5] was indeed legalised in many countries, and other countries like Canada prevented the unvaccinated from travelling via train, boat, or plane even after it had become clear that vaccination was not preventing infection or transmission of the virus. Of course, state officials did not deem these significant restrictions unfair on the basis that, since vaccination was widely available, being victim to these constraints was ultimately the result of people's own decisions. Accordingly, their servitude was voluntary. However, this logic begs the question of whether people actually had a genuine choice to make a free and enlightened decision when the price to pay for not conforming meant no longer being able to feed oneself or one's family. In Havel's Czechoslovakia, individuals were also free to refuse to adhere to the party line and to openly criticise their leaders. However, they were also fully aware of the impact their dissidence would have on their livelihood. How was this situation during the COVID-19 pandemic any different from the 1975 one the famous Czech dissident described? In both cases, freedom was only a theoretical notion as the pressure to abide by a specific state-oriented outcome was stronger than the willingness to resist. This is simply not what freedom ought to mean and seeing liberal societies taking that authoritarian shift was, to say the least, very worrying. But amazingly, a majority of people nonetheless welcomed these liberticidal measures. And, as I am planning to argue in this book, what is the most worrying about this episode is the fact that it was not just a sad momentary exception, but rather one that is part of a broader trend within liberal societies.

The question, then, is how these measures that now appear to have been disproportionate in light of the actual threat the virus posed were possible in the first place – because, yes, we now have the necessary distance at our disposal to make that claim without running the risk of being labelled as a conspiracy theorist. If in the early days and weeks of the pandemic, we may, because of a lack of scientific knowledge about the true nature of the virus, have been led to believe that this coronavirus was threatening to wipe out humanity, it nonetheless became quickly apparent to many scientists and health experts, thanks to clear data, that it was not the apocalypse many were forecasting. The lethality of the virus remained very low, and we quickly discovered that those who were the most susceptible to developing serious complications requiring medical care as well as to dying after contracting the virus were elderly people and individuals suffering from comorbidities

10 Introduction

Table I.1 Age of COVID-19-related deaths (New York City Health Department, as of May 13, 2020)

Age	Number of deaths	Share of deaths	With underlying conditions	Unknown if with underlying conditions	Without underlying conditions
0–17 years old	9	0.06%	6	0	3
18–44 years old	601	3.9%	476	108	17
45–64 years old	3,413	22.4%	2,851	490	72
65–74 years old	3,788	24.9%	2,801	982	5
75+ years old	7,419	48.7%	5,236	2,181	2
TOTAL	15,230	100%	11,370 (75%)	1,551 (24.7%)	99 (0.7%)

Source: Worldometers.info, www.worldometers.info/coronavirus/coronavirus-age-sex-demographics/

(see Table I.1) (di Stasio et al., 2020; Ebhardt et al., 2020; Minnai et al., 2022; Palmieri et al., 2020).[6] In fact, as of March 2021, only 689 people in England and Wales under the age of 60 years who had no known medical preconditions had died due to COVID-19, and the average age of those who died from the virus was 82.3 years.[7]

Accordingly, there is nothing inherently vile or unfair about the COVID-19 virus that has, for the most part, taken the lives of elderly individuals and only caused mild and momentary suffering for those who have decades ahead of them to express the potentialities of their lives. For instance, in the case of France – which is representative of cases elsewhere in the world – only 5% of those who died from the virus were (as of September 10, 2021) aged below 60 years, and those aged 0–9 years and 10–19 years each represented 0.01% of the overall number of victims. Those aged 20–29 years accounted for 0.1% of them, those aged 30–39 years accounted for 0.35% of them, and the age group 40–49 years represented 1% of them. This means that the total number of persons aged <60 years who died as a result of the virus (e.g. a total of 1,356 individuals) accounted for roughly two-thirds of the individuals under the age of 55 years who die annually in France in car accidents. Of course, this road fatality figure calls for measures to reinforce road safety and prevent dangerous driving; yet, no one is seriously suggesting that these data should lead the French state – apart from environmental motives – to ban automobiles from its territory. In the case of the pandemic, however, Western states have chosen the latter path: every death is now considered one too many and every mean must be deployed to prevent that from happening at all costs, even at the expense of people's freedom. That is what the sanctity of life implies.

Furthermore, despite causing the death of millions out of 619 million infected individuals – the official death toll reached 6.55 million as of October 5, 2022, though probably up to 16.6 million counting from the beginning of the pandemic to December 2022 according to estimates from the World Health Organization[8] (van Noorden, 2022) – the fact remains that this virus was nowhere near the tragedy many feared it would be and has been nowhere near comparable in proportion in terms of mortality to previous pandemics such as the medieval Black Death and the Spanish Flu during which a significantly higher proportion of people died from these diseases.[9] In fact, ranging from the most conservative to the most generous estimates, the COVID-19 pandemic killed between 0.08% and 0.20% of the world's population. Its death toll has, in fact, been rather similar to those of other twentieth-century pandemics that were almost forgotten prior to the Spring of 2020, namely the 1957–1958 Asian flu pandemic and the 1968 Hong Kong flu pandemic, which, respectively, caused the deaths of up to 4 million people. Based on the size of the global population at the time of each pandemic, the Asian flu killed 0.14% of the world population (then 2.9 billion), and the Hong Kong flu led to the death of 0.11% (3.5 billion). In hindsight, then, the COVID-19 pandemic was not novel and was ultimately a rather unexceptional situation that should have led to state implementation of preventive measures proportional to the danger posed; specifically, this should have entailed focusing on protecting the individuals most susceptible to dying from the virus in hospitals and nursing homes. However, this was not the case, and what was strikingly different in the case of the COVID-19 pandemic when compared with the Asian and Hong Kong flus was the extremity of the disproportionateness of the measures Western states imposed from 2020 until 2022. Western societies actually came to a complete halt without caring about the side effects these measures had, such as the dramatic increase in worldwide cases of domestic violence against women (Usta et al.,

2021), increased anxiety and depression,[10] long-term unemployment (Kelly, 2021), a sharp increase in the admission of children to psychiatric hospitals,[11] and the developmental delays caused in children (Wenner Moyer, 2022). People also tended to grossly overestimate the number of deaths that would result from this virus; among them was the Imperial College of London, which projected that 0.9% of people in Great Britain would die from the virus, whereas the actual number turned out to be 0.32% as of January 2023 (Adam, 2020). These exaggerated apocalyptic scenarios obviously influenced people. For instance, a survey conducted in July 2020 showed that British people thought that 7% of people in the United Kingdom had died from COVID-19. That proportion was 5% in France, 6% in Sweden, and 9% in the United States.[12] It is therefore not an overstatement to argue that Western states have grossly exaggerated the threat of this virus and adopted disproportionate measures dictated by the sole biological objective of saving lives (even if it paradoxically meant hindering in a dramatic way the quality of life of millions of people).

Why did Western societies overreact in 2020 in comparison with the two previous pandemics mentioned above? Something has clearly changed over the last 50 years, and this shift is associated with a growing fear of death and the fact that Western societies have now fully embraced the idea that lives have to be preserved at all costs. Of course, the logic that prevailed in Western societies was, in appearance, a noble one: since the world was facing an extraordinary health hazard, it was necessary to do everything possible to save as many lives as could be saved. French President Emmanuel Macron could not have said it better when he proclaimed – proudly, it must be added – that 'The unthinkable has happened! We have stopped the economy to save lives. We have finally decided to put humans at the centre of what really matters!'. In a similar vein, former German Chancellor Angela Merkel said, in March 2020, that the draconian measures the German government 'had to' impose were necessary to save lives, adding that it was nothing less than Germany's biggest challenge since the end of World War II (WWII). In August 2020, then presidential candidate Joe Biden reiterated the same mantra when he declared that he 'would be prepared to do whatever it takes to save lives'. Politicians who did not show the same enthusiasm for this logic

Introduction 13

were severely criticised by voters. This was, for instance, the case with former British Prime Minister Boris Johnson who warned the British people in the initial stages of the pandemic that they would have to take it 'on the chin' and be prepared to lose loved ones. Hence, 'saving lives at all costs' came to be hailed as the 'right' (and only) thing to do in the face of this deadly disease, triggering an unthinkable return to the dark ages of humankind when the logic justifying human sacrifices prevailed (Caron, 2022a).

Though noble in appearance, this logic that tends to perceive human life solely from a biological perspective is actually a perverted one that ends up limiting the expression of life itself – a sad perspective that simply increases the liberticidal measures imposed on people when existence is jeopardised by what is presented as a life-threatening menace. Indeed, when people feel that they are facing such a situation (that is when they are abiding by a purely biological understanding of life and when they are facing a deadly threat), they are placed in a perfect storm that results in serious limitations on their freedom: limitations they will welcome with open arms. I am not denying that extraordinary situations may rightfully lead to such outcomes, but this can only be justified when the challenge is indeed extraordinary and when the usual political tools at the state's disposal are not able to face it efficiently. The problem we are facing is that Western societies have gradually banalised these so-called life-threatening emergencies to a point where an increasing number of challenges and contingencies are now deemed to require the implementation of exceptional measures concomitant with the limitation of individual freedom. In other words, the state of emergency has become the new governance paradigm in these countries and, as a result, there has been declining concern for the protection of our liberties with the result that liberal societies are gradually becoming less liberal.

This brings us back to the question previously asked: Why were these disproportionate liberticidal measures possible and generally accepted by the people in so many liberal democracies, culminating in the imposition of a state of emergency that went beyond the time frame of any other similar situations from the past? I wish to emphasise in this book that the fear of dying – which is natural for any living creature, but which humans can and must nonetheless overcome – that has now taken over the collective psyche of people in Western societies was, until the last

30 years, subordinated to a conception of life built upon the defence of higher virtues, which made it possible to contemplate the biological aspect of life in a more relative way. This paradigm – profoundly Lockean in essence – has now disappeared and been replaced by a more primitive view that is closer to Hobbes' philosophical views and sees the value of life solely in its biological dimension. In light of its potential impacts on people's freedom, the lack of interest in this type of fear is a mistake since it possesses the potential to lead to liberticidal measures that are so significant in scope that they are probably the most menacing dangers currently threatening democratic societies and their citizens' freedom. It is therefore important to understand how the fear of dying has the potential to seriously transform the relationship between the state and its people in a way that is unfavourable to the latter's personal freedom. This is what this book will elucidate by exploring the origin of the fear of dying, its political impacts, and how it can be overcome (albeit, admittedly, not without significant difficulties).

What the COVID-19 pandemic has allowed us to see is the full impact of what had already been an evolutive trend among liberal democracies over the last few decades that went surprisingly unnoticed until the virus hit us. The fear of dying came full circle in the early Spring of 2020 when we realised, with great astonishment, that people had developed an irrational fear of death that had metamorphosed into the political belief that a single death is one too many that needs to be met by Chinese-like exceptional measures. When these fears occur, not only will people be willing to passively surrender their freedom to the state, but they will also be the ones requesting this form of servitude. If avoiding death and chaos has now become a fundamental axiom within Western societies and it is therefore of the utmost importance to understand why they have assumed such a role in our lives, considering how dangerous this trend is to our freedom.

Astana, March 2023

Notes

1 As was the case during the French Revolution, more specifically during the period of *terreur* that spanned 1793–1794, fear was not only a feeling 'traitors' experienced but was also experienced by individuals

who, in the words of Saint-Just, were deemed to be 'too passive' in their support of the Revolution (Caron, 2021a, 2023).

2 Abiding by a traditional vision of political tyranny premised on the idea that dissenting individuals *de facto* face arrest, torture, and death, Tocqueville also added the following:

> Princes had so to speak made violence material; democratic republics in our day have rendered it just as intellectual as the human will that it wants to constrain. Under the absolute government of one alone, despotism struck the body crudely, so as to reach the soul; and the soul, escaping from those blows, rose gloriously above it; but in democratic republics, tyranny does not proceed in this way; it leaves the body and goes straight for the soul. The master no longer says to it[, ']You shall think as I do or you shall die[']; he says[, ']You are free not to think as I do; your life, your goods, everything remains to you, but from this day on, you are a stranger among us. You shall keep your privileges in the city, but they will become useless to you; for if you crave the vote of your fellow citizens, they will not grant it to you, and if you demand only their esteem, they will still pretend to refuse it to you. You shall remain among men, but you shall lose your rights of humanity. When you approach those like you, they shall flee you as being impure; and those who believe in your innocence, even they shall abandon you, for one would flee them in their turn. Go in peace, I leave you your life, but I leave it to you worse than death'.
>
> (2000, p. 271)

3 In the words of John Stuart Mill:

> Like other tyrannies, the tyranny of the majority was at first, and is still vulgarly, held in dread, chiefly as operating through the acts of the public authorities. But reflecting persons perceived that when society is itself the tyrant – society collectively, over the separate individuals who compose it – its means of tyrannising are not restricted to the acts which it may do by the hands of its political functionaries. Society can and does execute its own mandates[,] and if it issues wrong mandates instead of right, or any mandates at all in things with which it ought not to meddle, it practices a social tyranny more formidable than many kinds of political oppression, since, though not usually upheld by such extreme penalties, it leaves fewer means of escape, penetrating much more deeply into the details of life, and enslaving the soul itself. Protection, therefore, against the tyranny of the magistrate is not enough: [T]here needs [to be] protection also against the tyranny of the prevailing opinion and

16 *Introduction*

> feeling; against the tendency of society to impose, by other means than civil penalties, its own ideas and practices as rules of conduct on those who dissent from them; to fetter the development, and if possible, prevent the formation, of any individuality not in harmony with its ways, and compel all characters to fashion themselves upon the model of its own.
>
> (2003, p. 76)

4 Austria introduced a law in February 2022 making vaccination mandatory on penalty of a fine but ultimately chose to suspend the mandate days before it was supposed to be enforced.

5 This was the case, for instance, at Western University, located in Canada, which made mask wearing and receipt of a third dose of a COVID-19 vaccine mandatory to access campus for the Fall 2022 semester. The University of California has also made vaccination (initial doses plus a booster) mandatory for its staff and students.

6 A vast study conducted in France has shown that, in comparison to people aged 45–54 years, individuals aged 85–89 years were four times more likely to be hospitalised and 38 times more likely to die after contracting COVID-19. Furthermore, only 10% of patients who were hospitalised because of COVID-19 and 2% who died from it did not have comorbidities. See 'COVID-19: chez les vaccinés, le risque de formes graves est lié à l'âge ou aux comorbidités, selon un vaste étude', www.lefigaro.fr/flash-actu/Covid-19-chez-les-vaccines-le-risque-de-for mes-graves-est-lie-a-l-age-ou-aux-comorbidites-selon-une-vaste-etude-20220211. Quebec's national institute of public health also reported that in the first months of the pandemic, 97% of those who died because of COVID-19 had at least one comorbidity and that 87% of individuals hospitalised due to COVID-19 also had at least one pre-existent medical condition. See www.inspq.qc.ca/sites/default/files/publications/ 3082-impact-comorbidites-risque-deces-Covid19.pdf, p. 1.

7 As of 2020, life expectancy in Britain was 80.9 years.

8 Simultaneously, however, there are reasons to be sceptical about these numbers as it has been revealed that many countries adopted a very generous way of counting deaths attributable to COVID-19 (e.g. those who died *because of* COVID-19 and those who died *with* COVID-19 were aggregated in the same category).

9 It is estimated that a third of the European population died of the bubonic plague during the fourteenth century, and the Spanish Flu killed 50–100 million people worldwide. Out of a population of 1.9 billion people at the time (in 1920), this means that nearly 5% of the global population died due to this virus.

10 A worldwide study published in October 2021 has shown that cases of depression rose by 53 million globally as a consequence of the pandemic (which corresponds to an increase of 28% compared with pre-pandemic levels), and cases of anxiety increased by 76 million (which corresponds to a 26% rise) (Santomauro et al., 2021).
11 'Covid-19: les hospitalisations en pédopsychiatrie ont explosé de 80%'. www.francetvinfo.fr/sante/enfant-ado/Covid-19-les-hospitalisations-en-pedopsychiatrie-ont-explose-de-80_4344365.html
12 www.kekstcnc.com/media/2793/kekstcnc_research_Covid-19_opinion_tracker_wave-4.pdf

1 Fear and the Meaning of Life

Social distancing, vaccination mandates, lockdowns, curfews, and *QR codes* – for two years, these words and expressions became part of most people's daily reality. Such a vocabulary was the result of people's fear of catching the COVID-19 virus. Consequently, a significant number of people literally stopped living normally by isolating themselves from their friends and family and limiting their movements to essential things, on top of adopting extreme hygienic behaviours as a means of protection.[1] In retrospect, all of this seems pretty absurd, especially on the part of young and healthy people with extremely low chances of dying from this virus in light of the data we now have at our disposal. Nevertheless, most of them complied with these liberticidal measures and thought that they were proportional to the threat they were facing even after it became clear that some of the measures were not scientifically justified. Vaccination mandates and passports that prevented unvaccinated individuals from travelling or entering some public places like restaurants and museums are good examples in this regard, as many such measures were repealed only months after it became clear that vaccination was not preventing transmission of the disease.[2] We could also mention the imposition of curfews at night, as if the virus was not circulating during the day.

Hence, this pandemic revealed that many individuals who were not actually susceptible to fatally succumbing to COVID-19 were gripped by their fear of dying – a fear so strong that it resulted in them completely halting their lives and passively accepting measures that hindered their freedom. This situation begs the question of why this fear of dying has become so significant to

DOI: 10.4324/9781003387749-2

many of us. Why have people adopted a purely biological conception of life, and what other sorts of policies can we expect to see in the future if this understanding of human existence remains the same, or worse, keeps gaining in popularity? These questions are far from trivial as the role that the fear of death is now occupying is actually symptomatic of a significant shift in our understanding of the meaning of politics – a shift that can only lead to the state's ever-growing interference in our lives and, consequently, limitation of our freedom.

My aim in this chapter is to identify the origins of this form of 'biopolitics' that tends to reduce human beings solely to their biological dimension. What is at stake here – and what this chapter will argue – is that even though the seeds that made the development of this conception of human life possible were planted a long time ago, many factors and contingencies have prevented it until very recently to have such an impact on us. We need, in this regard, to turn our attention to political modernity, which has resulted in the irreversible death of a conception of life that refuses to consider its biological component alone as being worthy of a truly human existence. In particular, a large contributor to this was the Enlightenment, which sanctified individuals' rights and their individual self-development as the supreme value of human existence and the primary obligation of states.[3] Of course, this shift in our comprehension of the essence of human existence had tremendous consequences that were clearly visible during the COVID-19 pandemic, namely, some individuals manifesting what I have called an irresponsible form of citizenship (Caron, 2021b) as well as engendering a valued type of existence that has made individuals highly vulnerable to being controlled by state authorities. This is what I will discuss in the first part of this chapter.

However, in spite of these problems, this impoverished understanding of what life ought to be did not result in our mere survival becoming paramount – what I call the *homo superstes* conception – even if the price is being subjected to liberticidal measures. This conception of life that has been so obvious during the COVID-19 pandemic is, on the contrary, a rather contemporary phenomenon and was kept in check until the end of the Cold War when it started to emerge as a dominant force in Western societies. Deriving from the need of liberalism to assert its value and superiority based on its opposition to a 'significant other', that is, the incarnation of what ought to be feared, I argue that the post-Cold War era has created a situation where its alterity was no longer based upon a different ideology, as was the case previously with communism and fascism, but rather upon the cruel and barbaric physical treatment and abuses to which individuals living in non-liberal societies were subjected. As such, the collective identity of individuals living in Western states ceased to be value-based as had previously been the case and instead became established on their capacity to ensure personal safety, of which others were, unfortunately, deprived in failed or rogue states. By establishing the liberal difference on this opposition to such inhumane political entities, Western societies have integrated within their collective psyche the idea that their most important task consists in ensuring the preservation of their members' lives – a view that is now, unlike in the previous periods when liberal exceptionalism was based on its ideological superiority, changing the relationship between individuals and their state in a way that has led to the creation of 'nannyism' logic, in which the state is no longer treating people as essential partners in the affirmation of liberalism's supreme goods but rather as entities that must be controlled. This is what the second part of this chapter will present.

The ancient Greeks had two different ways of describing life that referred to two very distinct realities, namely *zóé* and *bios*. In our times, we have been reminded of these realities by Michel Foucault (2004) and Hannah Arendt (1998), who evoked them in some of their works. Further, Italian philosopher Giorgio Agamben (1998) thoroughly discussed the subject. Whereas the former notion refers to natural life itself, which humans have in common with animals, the latter notion refers to the fact of converting natural life into what is inextricably associated with humans' uniqueness. According to their understanding of what politics was supposed to be about, that is, realising the ideal political system, Plato and Aristotle were only interested in the *bios* component of life. Indeed, because of humans' unique faculties, human society was thought to be distinctive from those of other living creatures because of humans' capacity to go beyond the simple natural existence and enjoy politics that allowed them to establish an ethical community – an outcome made possible by the common sharing of reason that allows individuals to make complex distinctions between what is right and what is wrong and not just express what is enjoyable or unpleasant through animal-like whining or purring. Though referring to an essential component of human life without which politics would not have been possible, the ancient Greeks were not associating human existence with the *zóé* type of life since it was not associated with what human life was meant to achieve; rather, it was linked with the essence of other species as can be exemplified by Aristotle's famous quote that men are nothing less than political animals.[4] For them, as for the Romans, such a life dedicated to one's biological existence was considered to be futile.

This distinction between these two conceptions of life has led to an understanding of the political sphere as a space aimed at achieving an ideal, as with Aristotle, where the realisation of human happiness (*eudaimonia*) is seen as the chief good (2000). This idealistic view of politics was the ultimate goal that humans had to follow individually and collectively. This sphere was therefore conceived as having nothing to do with elements connected with reproduction and subsistence that were rather relegated to the private sphere of *oikos*, which was completely disconnected from the Greeks' understanding of citizenship. Indeed, as a component of this private sphere, these elements of biological life were not deemed to have a place in the public sphere, which was rather conceived of as the sphere where individuals could elevate themselves to a superior level of political morality through dialogue. In other words, the opposition of *oikos* and *polis* was, in fact, reminiscent of two manners of conceiving human existence: 'to live' and 'to live well'. This is also why their understanding of a citizen was not (solely) associated with birth and was not considered to be a natural right, as well as why exile in the form of ostracism for those who were deemed to pose a threat to the state was one of the severest punishments that could have been imposed on a citizen. In light of their view on the value of human existence, denying an individual their right to play a role in the public sphere was akin to death, which is why choosing between being exiled from the Athenian polis and ceasing to be among other men or dying meant the same thing for Socrates.

Reminiscent of Arendt's view of *homo laborans*, the valorisation of the public sphere over the private one and the elevation of the idea of man as a political animal as the only genuine meaning of human existence was made possible in the Greek world thanks to different rules that allowed those who enjoyed the title of 'citizen' the capacity to be as divorced as possible from the considerations of subsistence and reproduction – activities that were akin to the nature of animals and therefore not intrinsically human. This meant, however, that the capacity to become a citizen whose actions in the public sphere were solely interested in the 'good life' and the common good meant having the capacity to not having to worry about the necessities of life. This is how the Greeks justified slavery[5] and the confinement of women to the private dimension of the household, as these were seen as necessary conditions for a few to enjoy citizenship (of course, at the expense of women and slaves, who were, accordingly, deprived of their humanity). From this perspective, far from being a way to increase profits, the exploitation of slaves was actually, for the Greeks, a way to liberate citizens from the rule of necessity that was perceived as being the essence of an animalesque life in order for them to be able to enjoy a truly unique human life.

These two spheres were therefore separated from one another as they entailed different activities that were intimately connected with two very distinctive ways of understanding life. Everything associated with the necessities of life, reproduction, and the preservation of human life was excluded from the political sphere, which was the only arena thought to allow for the full expression of human potentialities and the capacity to become a genuine human being. This is why biological life was subordinated to higher political goals, an approach that could not render people's lives a sacred reality, as is the case today. This also explains why these private matters were considered insignificant and unworthy of public attention since they were deemed contrary to the enjoyment of freedom and happiness. Strictly confining biological concerns to the private realm allowed for the development of a spirit of personal sacrifice as Pericles' famous funeral oration (*épitaphioi*) illustrates.[6] This idea derived directly from how they viewed the value of human existence, which resulted in their assertion that the immortal fame associated with people's sacrifices for their community's greater good had greater value than figuring out ways to extend one's lifespan as an end in itself. Because of the way the Greeks understood human life, dying 'like a man' was more meaningful than living 'like an animal', which is why the word *andres*, used to describe those who gave their lives in defence of their political association, means 'individuals who are fully humans' (qtd. in Loraux, 1986, p. 106). They viewed their activities in the public sphere as a way to leave behind a part of themselves, a heroic feat that was denied to slaves and individuals whose lives were entirely restricted to the private sphere and who were doomed to remain in obscurity.[7] The Greek polis or the Roman *res publica* allowed individuals to extract themselves from the futility of their biological life and act as humans, a thought Arendt summarised as follows:

> It is with respect to this multiple significance of the public realm that the term 'private', in its original privative sense, has meaning. To live an entirely private life means above all to be deprived of things essential to a truly human life[,] to be deprived of the reality that comes from being seen and heard by others, […] to be deprived of the possibility of achieving something more permanent than life itself. The privation of privacy lies in the absence of others; as far as they are concerned, the private man does not appear, and therefore it is as though he did not exist. Whatever he does remains without significance and consequence to others, and what matters to him is of no interest to other people.
>
> (1998, p. 58)

Nowadays, this distinction between the *zóé* and *bios* conceptions of life has disappeared with the advent of political modernity, which has led to a completely different understanding of politics that no longer sees this sphere as the space that ought to allow individuals to achieve superior moral ends. On the contrary, it is now assumed that what now matters the most – and what ought to be the state's primary objective – is ensuring people's capacity to live in accordance with their sense of authenticity and pursue a life dedicated to what makes them happy (with the right to life being essential to the satisfaction of one's conception of happiness). As a consequence, the ancient dynamic between the public and the private spheres has been completely abandoned and replaced by a view where the latter is superior to the former; this has come about through a radical shift in our understanding of what it means to be human. If, for the ancients, the answer to that question was being a political animal, it now means, from our modern viewpoint, being free to undertake any activity that will contribute to our individual happiness.

This individualistic revolution laid the groundwork for two perfectly perceivable realities during the pandemic. Firstly, by reinforcing the logic that our personal development and capacity to attain happiness are part of an entirely individual process that can be achieved independently of others, the Enlightenment not only undermined the value of citizenship but also led to its perception as a notion that can potentially hinder people's capacity to pursue their own chosen path of self-development. This relationship has now reached its paroxysm as individuals are no longer fearful of pitting themselves against their state and government whenever they believe that some rules or laws are hindering what they wish to do. If we go back in time, especially to the early days of the pandemic when we did not have a clear view of the dangerous nature and lethality of the virus, many governments introduced decrees that aimed at limiting individuals' freedom of movement to contain the virus as much as possible. When societies face such extreme and uncertain circumstances, it is not unreasonable to assume that a principle of precaution ought to be applied and that such restrictions on our freedom, insofar as they are meant to be as durationally limited as possible until we gain a clearer view of the situation, are justified. Such contingencies would therefore call on people to show what I have called elsewhere 'responsible citizenship' (2021b), that is, their capacity to accept that their individual freedom must be sacrificed when it genuinely poses a threat to other people's lives. However, contrarily, many people showed an irresponsible form of citizenship at the beginning of the pandemic by refusing to question the absolute nature of their negative freedom. Indeed, during the period of the great unknown in the Spring of 2020, individuals displayed behaviours that clearly demonstrated how the sense of community and the normal constraints that ought to be associated with common life are now perceived by many as obstacles to personal autonomy and freedom. For instance, at the peak of the health crisis in early March 2020, many Italians refused to obey the government's directive to abide by the law and stay at home. People felt that their negative freedom was more important than what was in the public interest, so the usual lines and crowds of people were still evident at Italian cafés and restaurants, and some people openly bragged about how they were able to have drinks with friends in establishments outside of the locked-down zones as a result of opting to travel on rural roads in order to elude police checkpoints (Horowitz & Bubola, 2020). In Canada, reports emerged of people who had tested positive for COVID-19 refusing to submit to the mandatory quarantine. Similarly, polls in countries deeply affected by the virus have shown the reluctance of numerous people to follow the recommendations of their public authorities. As an example, in March 2020, a Belgian poll showed that nearly 50% of people aged between 18 and 21 years were not respecting the confinement measures (overall, they accounted for 23% of the population). Even worse, the survey showed that only 24% of people who had experienced a symptom of the virus and 39% of those who had experienced at least two symptoms were respecting the strict confinement measures (RTBF, 2020). In France, the imposition of strict confinement measures in mid-March 2020 was met with some defiance; specifically, ten days after implementation of the measures, more than 225,000 people had already been fined for non-compliance (Sud-Ouest, 2020). These are just a few examples of irresponsible citizenship triggered by the popular belief that one's right to do what one wishes cannot be hindered by any other considerations, even considerations that any rational individual ought to have respected at a time (and it is important to emphasise this point) when the world was facing a lethal virus, the true nature of which was still unknown to a majority of global scientists.

These examples clearly show the disconnect between the judicial/philosophical logic of liberalism and the way many of us understand the exercise of individual freedom, as a significant number of citizens do not believe that limitations on their liberty are legitimate. As a result, by undermining the values, ideas, and sources of pride that once united people, this mentality has slowly eroded societies' common anchoring. All actions are now evaluated solely based upon what our own subjectivity dictates, with the consequence that our common world has ceased to exist. By emphasising people's right to authenticity, such an approach has encouraged them to emancipate themselves from all forms of power, which are currently perceived as heteronomous forces opposed to the expression of their autonomy. Consequently, dedication to religious beliefs or to secular ghosts like the nation is now more at odds with the dominant doxa. Similar to the way the main character in Albert Camus' *L'Étranger* (Meursault) is perceived by the other members of the community for not abiding by the usual norms, those who believe that people have a duty of loyalty to their community are now seen as strangers in a world in which these values are treated with suspicion as a potential threat to our freedom.

Secondly, as I have already discussed in the Introduction, the fear of losing one's job also led many individuals to abide by state policies during the pandemic despite the fact that some thought of them as being exaggerated. Although not apparent at first glance, this fear is also the result of political modernity and a clear sign of how the imperativeness of necessities that were, in the time of the Greeks, marks of the lowest form of human life, has shaped the current understanding of those necessities as constituting the most important component of modern life. Capitalism, a system unknown to the Greeks, has obviously majorly contributed to this evolution. Indeed, as Max Weber argued, ancient city-states were never centres of production, and the condition of slave owners had more to do with those of individuals of independent means (*rentier* in French) than with the capitalist, which is why Weber used the expression *pensionopolis* to describe these societies. From a similar perspective, Arendt wrote that

> [i]f the property-owner chose to enlarge his property instead of using it up in leading a political life, it was as though he willingly sacrificed his freedom and became voluntarily what the slave was against his own will, a servant of necessity.
> (1998, p. 61)

This logic allowed them to truly separate the public sphere from the necessities associated with *oikos*. This is no longer possible when work is thought to be the origin of everything humans ought to value, with one important aspect of it being a way for us to affirm ourselves in the highly anonymous and bureaucratic modern world. Indeed, even if the right to recognition is seen as a modern idea (Taylor, 1992), its need has always been present, and the ancients believed that it was achievable only through the public sphere, where individuals were able to display excellence (*aretè* for the Greeks and *virtus* for the Romans) to an audience of their equals (*homoioi*). The ancients' political system made it possible for them to gain that sort of recognition through the public realm. Because of the limitation on those permitted to participate, citizens' direct involvement afforded them the possibility to acquire the respect of their co-citizens by showing their usefulness and dedication to their society, with giving up their life being the ultimate sacrifice. In other words, only the public sphere facilitated the expression of their individuality.

The modern world has made this impossible. The public sphere is now a space occupied only by a few, who, with the help of a highly anonymous bureaucracy, have deprived citizens of their capacity to use it as a way to gain the recognition they desire. Through representative democracy, that sphere is open only to citizens when elections come, and for the rest of the time, policies are imposed by a legislative branch entirely under the control of a handful individuals belonging to the executive branch or by unelected civil servants. What we must realise here is that, despite the mass democratisation of Western societies, a phenomenon that has greatly extended citizenship rights beyond the ancients' restrictive rules, the number of individuals who are now able to use the public sphere to express their individuality and merits to others might actually be much smaller than it was in Athens. If we add to this reality the formidable forces of global capitalism that have confiscated a large segment of state sovereignty (*les pouvoirs régaliens de l'État*), the public sphere has now become a foreign reality to the masses. Inevitably, this separation from the sphere that ought to connect individuals beyond their individualities can only contribute to the aforementioned erosion of the sharing of a common citizenship and to the expansion of individualistic behaviours that can sometimes prove to be anarchic and dangerous for others. Indeed, if the public sphere was, for the Greeks and the Romans, the space where they were able to attain personal recognition, then it was a double-edged sword because it was also where they could lose it all and be denied their citizenship through ostracism – a punishment that, as I have argued, was seen as harsher than death because it condemned the individual to a non-human existence. However, in a world where the public sphere has lost all resonance in people's minds, the prospect of being publicly shamed for not displaying responsible citizenship does not have the same weight in people's minds; rather, people are inclined to shrug it off as an insignificant criticism and will even, in some cases, see merit in it.

From this perspective, in addition to the fact that, unlike the Greeks or the Romans, no one can expect to experience the life of a *rentier* in societies that have abolished slavery and made gender equality a non-negotiable gain, coupled with the reality that working to satisfy the necessities of life is an inescapable element of our existence, work is now, for many of us, the only means at our disposal to receive the recognition we are striving for, as well as a way that allows us to pursue what makes us happy. If, because of these changes to the way societies are organised, we can no longer avoid having to work in order to satisfy our basic needs, it would be a major mistake to neglect the fact that these two elements also constitute fundamental aspects of the work paradigm that now dictates our lives and explains why the fear of losing one's job makes us vulnerable to governments' decisions. In the first case, though acquiring recognition for personal merits was only achievable in ancient times through the public sphere, individuals now have the opportunity to receive this sort of gratification from others thanks to their work, which can take the form of a promotion or conferment of an award. In the latter case, work has also become, for modern people, inextricably connected with the development of their sense of authenticity, and it allows them to imbue their lives with purpose. This is, in a way, how Enlightenment philosophers perceived work, that is, as no less important than freedom of thought or opinion. Through liberation from the traditional feudal dependencies of the past, individuals are now thought to be able to express themselves through their individualised work (Kalyvas & Katznelson, 2008). In both cases, the attainment of recognition and self-affirmation through work implies the publicisation of the private sphere.

However, once individuals have fully integrated this view of work, a vicious circle in which this conception of happiness depends upon an understanding of their job is created that ends up enslaving people, since satisfying the former idea is not possible without the latter. As a result, individuals are facing a paradigm according to which the fear of losing their job constitutes no less than a personal tragedy as it is either the source or the condition of their well-being. When this is the case, societies – whether authoritarian or democratic – can easily control people's behaviours or thoughts simply by threatening that their nonconformity would result in employment-related consequences.

Fearful of losing what they perceive as the sole element contributing to their personal happiness, they have no alternative but to abide by the state's rules. This has been the case for many individuals whose decision to get vaccinated was the result of not wanting to lose their job after many employers made it a mandatory employment condition.

These factors have undoubtedly played a significant role in weakening the common political bounds, in the irresponsibility many showed in the early weeks of the COVID-19 pandemic, and in exposing people's vulnerability to being forced to comply with certain state rules. It is also certain that eliminating the distinction between the spheres of *oikos* and the public sphere, which the ancients held so dear, also allowed purely biological concerns to become political preoccupations, contributing to making the mere preservation of life a political obligation of the state.

However, these factors are unable in themselves to explain why these reactions were nothing compared to those people had during the previous pandemics in the second half of the twentieth century that did not lead to repetitive lockdowns and other liberticidal measures as we have witnessed during the COVID-19 pandemic or to a genuine fear of others as a potential threat to one's own life. Despite the threat of facing a potentially deadly virus, our parents and grandparents never resorted to such abusive measures. Why is this so? In the same vein, why were our ancestors from one or two generations ago willing to put their safety at risk and make sacrifices for their state despite having been reared in a modern world with principles no different from the ones that have dictated our own understanding of life? Something has managed to offset the powerful sources of biopolitics, something that is no longer present nowadays. But what is it?

From this perspective, the argument that the *homo superstes* conception of life that consists of surviving for as long as possible and now prevails in Western societies because of modernity is facing major criticism. Indeed, if the seeds of this purely biological view of life can be found in the Enlightenment, why did the extreme consequences of the *homo superstes* conception of life appear only recently and not 300 years ago? Many have argued (Beck, 1999; Bauman, 2000) that although the Enlightenment gave people their freedom, it nonetheless remained subordinated to a superior force that was either religious or secular, namely nationalism or ideology. The emergence of societies dominated by willingness to avoid risks that can threaten human life was only made possible when these religious and secular phantoms were disrupted following the 1960s 'rights revolution' that roundly sanctified the prevalence of individual freedom over any other considerations. As I have already argued elsewhere (Caron, 2020), this revolution was, in other words, the realisation of Max Stirner's dream as described in his book *The Ego and His Own* in which he famously criticises the failure of the Enlightenment to provide people with the pure and absolute freedom of serving only themselves. With this radical modernity, liberal societies have embarked on a revolutionary pattern that has led to the absolute sacralisation of individual rights in such a way that it has eliminated the connection between the individual and the community. Samuel Walker described this shift as follows:

> This revolution includes a broad array of formal rights codified in laws and court decisions; but even more important, it involves a new rights consciousness, a way of thinking about ourselves and our society. As some observers point out, this new 'rights culture' is marked by an almost reflexive habit of defining all problems in terms of rights. The words, expressed as demands, fall quickly from our lips: 'I have a right to ....'. These rights include an expectation of personal liberty, freedom from unwarranted government regulation of both public and private matters, a right to speak freely on public affairs, and a freedom to conduct our private – including [and] especially our sexual – lives as we choose.
>
> (1998, p. vii)

Being deprived of the capacity to identify with anything higher than themselves has certainly contributed to the decline of common bonds and people's willingness to adjust their actions in accordance with what I have called responsible citizenship, but it has also been argued that it left individuals unable to project themselves beyond their mere rights, with the most important being their right to life. Consequently, this is deemed to have started the transition to post-heroic societies fundamentally defined by their aversion to risks that might jeopardise people's lives, health, or well-being.

This was also one of Alexander Solzhenitsyn's main criticisms of the Western world in his famous 1978 Harvard speech in which he severely criticised the fact that civic courage has disappeared from Western societies. If, in his view, the Enlightenment allowed people to enjoy their freedom and capacity to pursue happiness, the post-WWII evolutions of liberalism have engendered a pattern that has led to the creation of a system where the state is solely responsible for ensuring people's material well-being and their personal independence from any form of interference and discrimination through a legal framework that ignores the general interest and focuses solely on individuals' rights. Inevitably, such a way of thinking has led to the general spiritual decay of ideals like courage that require subordination of our personal interests to a higher goal. In this context, he wondered the following:

> The individual's independence from many types of state pressure has been guaranteed; the majority of the people have been granted well-being to an extent their fathers and grandfathers could not even dream about; it has become possible to raise young people according to these ideals, preparing them for and summoning them toward physical bloom, happiness, the possession of material goods, money, and leisure, toward an almost unlimited freedom in the choice of pleasures. So who should now renounce all this[?] [W]hy and for the sake of what should one risk one's precious life in defense of the common good and particularly in the nebulous case when the security of one's nation must be defended in an as yet distant land?
>
> (1979, pp. 13, 15)

Although I agree with this point to some extent – in that this phenomenon has certainly contributed to the erosion of a sense of common citizenship and the irresponsible behaviours many showed at the beginning of the pandemic – as I have argued in previous works (Caron, 2020, 2021b), the question is how it has impacted the development of a *homo superstes* conception of life, since there was a significant delay between the appearance of this latter logic with the rights revolution and the sanctification of individual rights some 30 years before. During that period of time, the subordination of personal interests to a higher political goal – these 'secular ghosts' – which often required sacrifices from individuals, remained a feature of political life. Indeed, the 1970s and the 1980s were still heavily marked by an ideological battle with communism on the political front, while nationalism was the driving force behind political mobilisation elsewhere, such as in Quebec, Scotland, and Flanders. Without denying that the rights revolution may have had an impact on our contemporary understanding of life based on its purely biological meaning, I do believe that we may have to look in another direction in order to identify the more recent reason the *homo superstes* conception of life is so present in our lives.

The question is as follows: What caused this delayed reaction in the development of the full-blown *homo superstes* conception of life that now prevails? I believe that an explanation can be found in liberalism becoming the 'only ideological game in town' ever since its default victory over communism more than 30 years ago. In other words, the fall of communism (which was preceded some 50 years before by liberalism's victory over fascism, its other existential twentieth-century enemy) has led to a situation that has eliminated the great ideological threats liberalism had to face during the twentieth century by creating a political environment devoid of any valuable and credible political alternatives. More precisely, this lack of a competitor for liberalism left a major void that had to be filled somehow – with another form of fear that could serve as a mirror of an alterity to be avoided. It is, in other words, liberalism's 1991 victory that caused its own decay over the last 30 years and allowed states – due to people's fear of dying – to so easily implement liberticidal policies. Francis Fukuyama's celebration of liberalism as the 'end of history' has, in fact, opened a Pandora's box that has paradoxically led to the erosion of liberal values and principles in Western societies – a process we can now fully understand, thanks to the COVID-19 pandemic.

It must be said that, despite its significant drawbacks, fear also serves important social and political functions. Apart from the previously discussed role it plays in ensuring peace, order, and stability within political associations, a small dose of fear can be highly beneficial to societies as it helps develop well-needed social virtues, namely, vigilance and the willingness to protect and defend institutions that allow people to be free and enjoy basic human rights. In contrast, when individuals are no longer fearful, there is a risk that they might lower their guard and develop a form of social apathy that can only lead to the idea of personal comfort overcoming any other social consideration to the point where people stop seeing any value in personal sacrifice for the greater good. For St. Augustine, it is precisely this lack of vigilance caused by a lack of fear (which led to *apatheia*) on the part of Roman citizens that favoured the conflicts between Marius and Sulla and Pompey and Caesar. After all, as Richard Nixon argued, 'People respond more to fear than love', a reality 'they do not teach you in Sunday school' (PBS, 1992). Montesquieu shared a similar opinion about the social usefulness of fear. He saw in despotism, described as a state of affairs where individuals are brutalised, tortured, and killed solely for the tyrant's pleasure, an amazing deterrent for people living in free societies. Indeed, when people in non-despotic regimes are aware of how terrible things are elsewhere, it incentivises them to close ranks and defend and protect their freedom based on awareness of the potential consequences of not doing so. This feeling of having a clear and present enemy whose values and principles are inherently detrimental to what is presented as our superior mode of living serves as a catalyst for devotion to the common good that can go as far as motivating individuals to sacrifice their lives. This was, in essence, mentioned in the funeral speech Pericles gave to his fellow Athenians in which he clearly indicated the superiority of their model of governance and why it was worthwhile and even desirable to die to preserve it – a sacrifice that merited the city's highest honours. However, the success of this vision of fear requires the actual presence of an enemy who will act as a mirror of what we do not want to look like and thus as a fortifying fear that will mobilise our faith in ourselves as well as our willingness to affirm who we are and for what we stand. In other words, it is assumed that ideologies, civilisations, and great ways of thinking are unable, by themselves, to generate a faith sufficiently strong to enable believers to show a combative spirit. From this perspective, a period of peace when people are no longer facing an enemy is no longer conducive to this type of affirmation of values. In other words, you can only understand what makes you unique and how your state's policies are thought to be superior through comparison with others. During the Cold War, the 'Red Scare' was so effective at uniting Americans that they came to believe that any idea opposed to individualism, equality of opportunity, and personal freedom was completely alien to them and the opposite of the American creed (Hartz, 1955). Self-reflecting on one's identity without benefitting from external references and pondering the value of one's state institutions with respect to what they stand for in theory are arduous tasks. This is what Judith Skhlar's (1989) notion of the 'liberalism of fear' refers to – managing to unite individuals living in such societies around an immediate common understanding of who they are collectively by exposing them to a repulsive alternative view of what they could become; for Westerners living in liberal democracies, this repulsive alternative is the fear of human cruelty that has become perceived as the absolute evil to be fought.

Liberalism's self-definition as an ideology that primarily favours the full expression of people's freedom has, unsurprisingly, led Western states to adopt policies aimed at preventing individuals from falling victim to discrimination that limits their genuine capacity to empirically enjoy equal rights. Indeed, by granting universal and equal individual rights, the 'rights revolution' has given the false impression that all individuals have an equal chance to empirically fulfil their own conception of happiness. This is not the case, however, as social norms are not culturally neutral and may thus prevent individuals belonging to minority groups from enjoying the same rights as those who belong to the dominant ethnocultural group. For instance, requirements such as a specific, mandatory uniform for the police and armed forces, including a photo on one's driving license, and refraining from bringing weapons to school are all rules that have been considered discriminatory by members of religious or cultural minorities who have argued that such rules prevent them from enjoying their right to religious/cultural freedom. Attempting to prevent such a situation from occurring, philosopher Charles Taylor (1992) defended the necessity of implementing a 'politics of difference' in liberal societies, which entails granting derogations from common rules. This differentiated treatment is considered to be a way for those affected by discrimination caused by the false neutrality of public norms to have an equal right to religious/cultural freedom. In such cases, this treatment is not meant to offer special privileges to ethnocultural and religious minorities. Rather, it is an equalisation tool that makes the enjoyment of rights a practical reality instead of a symbolic fiction. This is why Sikhs are allowed to wear their ceremonial *kirpan* in some public places and can wear their turban instead of the traditional headwear dictated by their profession, such as the conventional police hat, the military beret, or the wig worn by barristers and judges in some countries. Such differentiated treatment is not granted only to ethno-cultural or religious minorities. Indeed, it has also been given to individuals who, because of their socio-economic situation, also see the impairment of some of their fundamental rights. This is why court-appointed lawyers are often provided free of charge to individuals whose income is below a certain level. Indeed, without such treatment, the right of individuals, namely poor individuals, to a fair and equal trial would remain entirely theoretical, as they would not otherwise have the resources to hire a competent lawyer to defend them, unlike individuals who have substantial financial assets. Since economic disparities between individuals can cause discrimination and the incapacity of some to enjoy equal rights, such differentiated treatment is necessary and should be seen solely as a tool for equalising rights. A genuine understanding of liberalism will therefore require accepting these exceptions. Western states have accordingly seen an explosion of differentiated treatment since the 1980s and what we are witnessing now with movements such as Black Lives Matter, LGBTQ2S+, and other requests linked with what is called 'identity politics' is simply an extension of the legacy of the Cold War concept of the 'liberalism of fear' that has defined itself as a regime opposed to the cruelty of not being able to fully enjoy one's freedom.

Denying people the possibility to affirm the value of their cause through a confrontation with the 'other' leads individuals to take what they have for granted and devalue greater common ideals, such as personal sacrifice, in favour of refocusing their interest on their own private affairs. This is exactly what happened to the liberal world following the end of the Cold War: Deprived of its ideological alterity, Westerners gradually forgot who they were and the value of that for which they stood. Unsurprisingly, many worried about this prospect; indeed, numerous post-1991 statesmen and philosophers explicitly worried about the consequences of no longer being able to compare the value of liberal democracies with a 'significant other', an essential task not only for our capacity to understand who we are and what we stand for but also for generating civic engagement. Indeed, if our differences (and, correlatively, our superiority) can be highlighted by comparing ourselves with others on an individual or collective basis, such comparison also contributes to creating what can be (but is not necessarily) a healthy type of fear by leading us to understand what we could lose, thereby generating in us a desire to actively defend our way of life. This latter feature was clearly present during the Cold War in a way that has been completely different ever since the collapse of the Soviet Union. This evolution explains the present-day dominance of a purely biological understanding of human existence, as I will explain more thoroughly in Chapter 2.

What replaced the previous opposition with communist tyranny was therefore the result of that period's contingencies and was established around the value of liberalism as an ideology that favoured the safety of people contrary to rogue and failed states like the former Yugoslavia or Rwanda, where thousands of individuals were mercilessly massacred in front of the world's cameras. The liberalism of fear therefore became established as the opposite of regimes built on the fear of being killed or maimed, thus serving as a mirror that allows people to understand the value and meaning of a limited coercive government that aims to prevent others from harming us. What makes this understanding easy to grasp is the fact that the fear of falling victim to cruel treatment is so natural in our psyche that individuals do not need to be convinced of the need to reject cruelty based on some deep philosophical thinking; they can recognise it immediately as a non-negotiable principle of political morality. This is why, in the post-Cold War era, the basic norm of the political practices and prescriptions of liberalism became the fear of falling victim to physical violence. More precisely, the superiority of the Western world became understood as its capacity to ensure personal safety in a world plagued by death, cruelty, inhumane treatment, genocide, and other types of large-scale suffering. Hence, this alterity differed significantly from the one that prevailed in the previous decades, and its consequences regarding the types of fear that derived from it, as well as the nature of people's relationship with their state, were completely different and swung the door wide open for a *homo superstes* conception of life. When communism showed its potential for physical violence, such as in 1956 during the Hungarian uprising or through the Gulag system, such violence was not its primary defining figure in the West; rather, the main image was the regime's inability to guarantee people's freedom and its willingness to destroy people's souls.[8] The Cold War opposition between 'us and them' was therefore value-based primarily around the idea of freedom, whereas post-Cold War liberalism was put in opposition to murderous regimes and, as a result, replaced the centrality of freedom with the preservation of life, a feeling fuelled by the terrible fact that the murderous nature of liberalism's alternative had become visible for the first time through live reports shown on television depicting the heinous events in Bosnia and Rwanda. Consequently, the fear of dying became a determinant feature of Westerners' lives and replaced what was previously the fear of political oppression at the heart of what they stood for and their self-conception in general. The fact that, with the end of the Cold War, liberalism was no longer considered a project for the perfectibility of humankind but rather a mere instrument of survival was by no means an insignificant shift as it now explains multiple aspects of how Western societies are currently organising themselves in the wake of facing challenges.

The political ramifications of this new alterity for the liberal West took many forms in the post-Cold War era under the umbrella of the paradigm of human security organised around two main thrusts, namely 'freedom from fear' and 'freedom from want'. Whereas the first pillar sought to find ways to limit the impact of war and conflicts on people, the second one aimed at eliminating the other non-violent threats to human security like hunger and disease. More precisely, the agenda of freedom from fear prevented political entities from becoming failed states and enabled peace building and the prevention of human rights violations on a massive scale, such as genocide or ethnic cleansing, thus avoiding experiencing the traumatic situations seen in Rwanda and Srebrenica, where Western states did not act to prevent people from getting killed. This took many forms, such as the 1997 signing of the International Convention banning landmines – one of the most indiscriminate weapons of warfare – and the North Atlantic Treaty Organization's (NATO) 1999 military intervention in Kosovo, which was the prelude to the 2005 adoption of the 'responsibility to protect' (R2P) principle. In other words, in the post-1991 era, the mirror of political liberalism stopped being the existential threat totalitarian regimes posed to people's freedom and was replaced by a visceral fear of dying – a paradigm that gained further importance in people's minds following the 9/11 terrorist attacks. Indeed, whereas communism was, for the most part, the incarnation of a regime that was first and foremost inimical to individual freedoms, terrorism stands for the indiscriminate and large-scale targeting of people who have done nothing to justify their loss of immunity to a violent death (Caron, 2023). With this new form of political violence, what is at stake is no longer a way of life but rather life itself, which has come under threat at the hands of an elusive and murderous enemy hiding in the shadows and waiting to strike against us – anyone of us actually – when we are least expecting it.

Inevitably, this way of defining the value of liberalism comes with many problems. The first one is certainly the fact that it is a reductionist approach to politics. Unlike the previous way of assessing liberalism that, during the Cold War period and before, when the free world was at war against Nazism, was value-based on the superiority of a way of life and on explicit ideas, namely freedom, the right to private property, the right to pursue happiness, and the right to privacy, its post-1991 justification opened up a completely different relationship between the state and its people. In the previous paradigm, preserving these values was conducive to civic engagement as people knew that their freedom depended on their duty to be politically active even if it was for a purely utilitarian purpose. Indeed, the state alone cannot defend these forms of freedom; rather, in times of crisis or war, their preservation requires the active support of people who will be expected to make sacrifices for their defence. Life, according to its biological understanding, that is, surviving, was therefore not an absolute notion in the Cold War paradigm. Instead, it was subordinated to the importance of acting when necessary to preserve the supremacy of that for which the society stood. Consequently, despite having strong individualistic roots, the ideological struggles inherent to modern societies have, nonetheless, been able to control people's selfishness by keeping alive a form of active and heroic life. As such, it would be a mistake, in my view, to say that the effective victory of life understood from its *zóé* viewpoint rather than from its *bios* conception was fully accomplished with the Enlightenment. Because of the way the 'liberalism of fear' was conceptualised during the Cold War, the value of biological life nonetheless remained subordinated to other imperatives with the result that life was not completely sacred and understood as the supreme value societies had to be preserved by all means. In this regard, although the necessary foundations for the emergence of a risk society may have been planted during the 1960s rights revolution, its rise was hindered for many decades because of how the essence and meaning of liberalism were primarily framed thanks to its dystopian ideological mirror. This 'liberalism of fear' therefore acted as a force suppressing individualism by managing to make the enjoyment of personal freedom dependent upon the survival of the liberal way of life, thereby generating the meaning of personal sacrifices and overshadowing the idea that life means more than its mere biological process. In this case, the *homo libertas* understanding of life was conducive to its transformation into a *homo sacrificium* understanding, characterised by ideas that are more and more foreign to individuals who experienced their entire adult life after the end of the Cold War and who grew up with the post-1991 version of that to which liberalism compares itself.[9]

This evolution can be observed through the evolution of social mobilisations that have gradually shifted their focus away from what I have called 'sacrificial fights' in favour of 'life-threatening apocalyptic fights' (Caron, 2022a). This can be observed, in my opinion, by analysing how support for causes associated with struggles for national liberation – most likely, the best marker of people's willingness to agree to make sacrifices – has evolved over the last few decades. In some cases, support for such causes has dramatically waned over time. An example is the Quebec secessionist movement that saw its support rise from 40% during the 1980 referendum on sovereignty to 49.4% in the second referendum of 1995. However, over the last 25 years, the movement to realise Quebec's independence has seen its support waned.[10] A key feature of this decline is the fact that Parti Québécois' electoral basis has not been renewed with members of the young generation, as many youth are opposed to secession or simply do not see it as a priority.[11] As a result, the struggle for secession is dying, with its supporters, who are getting older, meeting the same fate. In the last elections held in October 2022, the party received a mere 14.6% of the votes, and only three candidates managed to be elected – a historical low for the party since its creation in 1967.

What can explain the desertion of this cause? One of the reasons explaining this growing dissatisfaction with the 'sovereigntist option' is the belief that independence will incur serious negative economic consequences, an explanation that is hardly surprising considering that the idea of sacrifice – even if the sacrifice may be life-threatening or damaging to one's well-being – has ceased to play an important part in people's lives.[12] However, in a world where fear has been organised around an idea, namely the fear of oppression, this 'sacrificial fight' is, nonetheless, worth it in the eyes of many who believe (rightly or wrongly – this is not the question here) that the Canadian state is, in fact, a colonial and oppressive system that denies Quebecers' right to self-determine freely.

However, we should not ignore the way young people's political involvement has metamorphosed over time, highlighting how the *homo superstes* conception of existence has overtaken the notion of sacrifice that played a big part in their parents' and grandparents' view of life. Indeed, the young generation's dedication to political causes is now largely dictated by a possible environmental cataclysm associated with climate change. What is now called 'eco-anxiety' arises from knowledge of the idea that extreme weather phenomena, the loss of biodiversity, increased pollution, overexploitation of natural resources, and rising sea levels may have harmful implications, which is why those suffering from it tend to be afflicted with stress, anxiety, nervousness, insomnia or sleep deprivation, depression, and other mental health-related issues. Studies have, indeed, shown how dramatically the climate crisis is affecting young people's mental well-being. For instance, a September 2021 survey conducted in ten countries with more than 10,000 respondents aged 16–25 years showed that the majority of respondents perceived themselves as having no future because of the climate crisis (75%) and believed that humanity is doomed (56%).[13] Feelings of fear and anxiety owing to this situation are so serious among young people that 39% of the respondents questioned the good sense of having children in a world that was, according to them, about to collapse and would, accordingly, plunge any future generation into hazardous living conditions. Death, or, rather, the fear of dying due to polluted water or air, plays a dominant role in young people's lives today, which is why the environmental question will soon become the top-most priority in Western societies,[14] as if the degradation of our environment is a novelty that eclipses how, in the previous century, the industrial revolution in technologically advanced nations also led to severe and irremediable habitat damage. What explains this sudden awareness and call for action can only be attributed, in my view, to the way people have gradually started to understand the meaning of human existence in the last few decades. With our understanding of human existence no longer opposed to political oppression but rather premised on the fear of dying, we should not be surprised to see how the former importance of the good fight has waned in favour of 'life-threatening apocalyptic' involvements such as the fight against climate change, a cause that bears no similarity to any of the previous battles. Furthermore, it is also understandable that these latter mobilisations are, for the most part, led and fuelled by young activists from the post-1991 generation whose lives have never been exposed to the same forms of totalitarianism their elders experienced. Having come of age in a post-1991 world, their mindset is rather post-heroic as one would expect from individuals whose life conception is dominated by the fear of death; as a result, they are, unlike their parents and grandparents, less prone to favour liberal values (Foa & Mounk, 2016) and to subordinate them to what many of them consider to be a greater good, namely remaining alive.

If contemporary social mobilisations can provide us with a useful glimpse of the new reality in which Western societies are living when it comes to our understanding of human existence, then the way wars and human losses are now assessed is another very useful indicator. We have now entered the era of 'zero-death warfare ethics', where states are displaying maximal efforts to minimise as much as possible the dangers to which their soldiers are exposed. We are, indeed, a far cry from previous conflicts when it was not unusual to witness the complete destruction of entire units in only a few minutes.[15] The success of a military operation is now largely calculated based on the human cost it entails (on 'our side', of course) as well as the state's capacity to maintain its populace's support. Indeed, nowadays, the level of tolerance for the death of our soldiers during these missions has reached a historical low. Furthermore, the death of only a handful of soldiers can generate a significant decline in citizen support for a mission. Indeed, people will no longer accept the sacrifice of thousands of soldiers before questioning the war effort. Only a handful of fallen combatants may lead to a shift in public opinion, which further reinforces the (strange and counterintuitive) idea of war as a sanitised project that should not entail the death of soldiers. For instance, regarding

Canada's involvement in Afghanistan, support for the mission in March 2006 reached 55%, while 41% of Canadians opposed it, according to a poll. Moreover, three-fourths of the respondents said they had no emotions regarding the mission (those who reported emotions were less supportive of the mission). At the time this survey was conducted, Canada had lost eight soldiers (four of them having been killed by friendly fire when an American F-16 mistook them for insurgents and dropped a bomb, an accident now known as the Tarnak Farm incident). However, after the armed forces' redeployment to Kandahar, the number of fallen soldiers quickly accelerated and eventually reached a total of 158 in 2014, when Canada formally withdrew its military from Afghanistan. From 2006 to 2007, public support for the mission quickly eroded when flag-draped caskets started to arrive in Canada at regular intervals, even though a majority of Canadians agreed that the intervention aimed for noble objectives. More precisely, 55% believed that Canada's presence in Afghanistan was important to limit opium production, and 81% believed that premature withdrawal would negatively affect women's rights. However, despite people's endorsement of the government's view of the mission, their support was overshadowed by the emotional response they had as a result of what was considered an unacceptable number of fatally wounded soldiers, which proved stronger than any other human value.[16] This phenomenon was not precipitated by thousands of causalities; all it took was the death of a few soldiers in Afghanistan.

This view is also behind the idea of 'clean wars' and new privileged means of fighting enemies that have radically transformed soldiers' risk of death. Indeed, killing during warfare has always been justified by the fact that the risk of death is reciprocal. It is according to this logic that soldiers have been absolved of any wrongdoings for killing their foes, since the death of the latter was seen as the result of the former's right of self-defence (Walzer, 2006). Consequently, this dynamic between soldiers has often been compared to a duel where both parties are wilfully exposing themselves to the risk of being harmed or killed. War was, from this perspective, heroic. Nowadays, the relationship between opposing soldiers has changed dramatically, with Western states resorting to new methods of warfare that are removing their combatants from the battlefield by allowing them to fight the enemy remotely using the most well-known weapon among unmanned vehicles, commonly referred to as a drone. Although I am not questioning the importance of the military's duty of care towards its members (Caron, 2019b), the problem with these new weapons is that they are creating the condition Paul W. Kahn (2002) has labelled 'riskless warfare', where soldiers using these weapons benefit by gaining immunity from being killed. Consequently, war is transforming from duelling into manhunting (Chamayou, 2015) and, by doing so, has ushered in a post-heroic reality that is a very recent trend within Western societies.

Conclusion

These are, to my thinking, the origins of the *homo superstes* understanding of life – but what about its consequences? I believe that the most important one is the fact that, unlike the previously dominant fear of fascist or communist oppression, the fear of death no longer requires people's active participation in the public realm or their desire to keep the powers of the state in check out of fear that its actions might result in their loss of freedom. On the contrary, this task can be solely accomplished by the state and its representatives, and, in return, citizens are now fully expecting such actors to solely fulfil that role. This fundamental change in the dynamic between the state and its people is the source of the second problem: citizens' never-ending demand for their state to implement measures that will enable them to remain safe from any danger. Once this dynamic is in place, the risk of seeing the state implement liberticidal policies is very high since the main imperative has shifted from freedom to protection, two notions that are mutually exclusive, with the latter having the potential to seriously hinder the former. In fact, protective measures will be demanded, welcomed, and praised by the people themselves despite the impact they may have on their freedom, since that principle has now been eclipsed by their desire to avoid death. This is how the *homo superstes* understanding of life has taken root as a conception of human existence that gives the highest importance to people's physical well-being rather than the defence of ideas, with the result of shrinking individuals' political spirituality down to their sole biological essence, as well as devaluing self-sacrifice as an act that falls outside the realm of politics. Contrary to the previous manner in which liberalism understood itself through its superiority to communism and fascism, Western societies have been witnessing, since the end of the Cold War, a total reversal of values in terms of what it now means to be human, with one major consequence being their evolution into post-heroic societies that are unable to generate support for any value-based causes. As an outcome of the way liberalism now perceives itself and its distinctiveness, heroism – even if it is for instrumental reasons – is no longer possible as the entire notion of sacrifice has become self-contradictory, since it now requires individuals to sacrifice their lives for the sake of not dying. As a result, this new paradigm is also intimately connected with the creation of what can be called 'political nannyism'; that is, the political vision has been entirely devoted to ensuring people's physical well-being and preservation from any dangers that can harm them. This is what Chapter 2 will discuss.

Notes

1 I think that we have all seen individuals wearing a mask while sitting alone in their car and even people wearing (at the same time) a mask, a facial shield, and protective gloves. Personally, I even saw an individual wearing a WWI gas mask in the fruit section of my local grocery store as well as numerous individuals screaming at others (and even resorting to physical violence) for not respecting social distancing or for not wearing a mask properly above their nose.
2 This was the case in Canada, which finally abolished this obligation in June 2022; the mandatory 14-day quarantine for unvaccinated travellers was removed only a few months later in October 2022.
3 Article 2 of the 1789 Declaration of the Rights of Man and of the Citizen states: 'The goal of any political association is the conservation of the natural and imprescriptible rights of man'.
4 In *The Politics*, he writes:

> But obviously man is a political animal in a sense in which a bee is not, or any other gregarious animal. Nature, as we say, does nothing without some purpose; and she has endowed man alone among the animals with the power of speech. Speech is something different from voice, which is possessed by other animals also and used by them to express pain or pleasure; for their nature does indeed enable them not only to feel pleasure and pain but to communicate these feelings to each other. Speech, on the other hand serves to indicate what is useful and what is harmful, and so also what is just and what is unjust. For the real difference between man and other animals is that humans alone have perception of good and evil, just and unjust, etc.
> (1962, p. 60)

5 Arendt argued that

> The institution of slavery in antiquity, though not in later times, was not a device for cheap labor or an instrument of exploitation for profit but rather the attempt to exclude labor from the conditions of man's life. What men share with all other forms of animal life was not considered to be human.
> (1998, p. 84)

6 Which reads

> I believe that a death such as theirs has been the true measure of a man's worth; it may be the first revelation of his virtues, but is at any rate their final seal. [...] They resigned to hope their unknown chance of happiness; but in the face of death they resolved to rely upon themselves alone. And when the moment came[,] they were [re]minded to resist and suffer, rather than to fly and save their lives; they ran away from the word of dishonor, but on the battlefield their feet stood fast, and in an instant, at the height of their fortune, they passed away from the scene, not of their fear, but of their glory. [...] Wherefore I do not now pity the parents of the dead who stand here; I would rather comfort them. You know that your dead have passed away amid manifold vicissitudes; and that they may be deemed fortunate who have gained their utmost honor, whether an honorable death like theirs, or an honorable sorrow like yours, and whose share of happiness has been so ordered that the term of their happiness is likewise the term of their life.
> (Thucydides, 1974, Book 2, chap. 6)

It must also be added that the aforementioned strict separation between the private and the public spheres was also clearly visible during these public funerals. As Nicole Loraux noted, such events were reserved for men, and women's role was clearly restricted to sequestration with the parents of the deceased; their presence was not allowed in the official procession (only afterwards at the tomb) (1986, p. 24).

7 In this regard, Aristotle wrote in his *Nicomachean Ethics* that not because we are mortals should we care only about matters of life and death; rather, we should take on the quest for immortality as much as possible and act to live in accordance with our unique human potentialities (2000, 1177b).

8 This was, of course, a mistake, as communist dictatorships have led to the death of tens of millions of individuals. However, as Alexander Solzhenitsyn argued, the murderous nature of communism has been attributed to individuals such as Stalin or to the incorrigible tendency

and hereditary evil of the Russian people. As he has pointed out, many influential American scholars, like Robert Tucker, held this view and argued that Stalin's infamous acts were not the result of his Marxist views but rather of Russia's past (1980).
9 Empirical studies have also shown that support for liberal values, such as the protection of key rights and civil liberties, has experienced a sharp decline amongst millennials (individuals born after 1980) in comparison with their baby boomer parents (born in the first two decades after WWII). Though 41% of baby boomers believe that it is 'absolutely essential' for a democracy to protect people's liberty, that share has fallen to 32% of millennials (Foa & Mounk, 2016).
10 The political party that has historically promoted this option, Parti Québécois, has seen its support decline consistently over the last 25 years. It went from commanding 43% of the votes in the 1998 provincial elections (with 76 of 125 seats in the National Assembly) to securing 17% of the votes (and only ten seats) in the 2018 elections.
11 An October 2020 survey showed that, whereas 40% of respondents aged 55 years and above were in favour of Quebec's secession, the proportion declined to 34% among those aged 34–55 years and 31% among those aged 18–34 years.
12 The same factor was found to be decisive regarding young Scots' support for independence. See Jason Allardyce, 'Young Scots "will change vote" if prosperity at risk', *The Times*, May 9, 2021.
13 Caroline Hickman, Elizabeth Marks, Panu Pihkala, Susan Clayton, Eric Lewandowski, Elouise E. Mayall, Britt Wray, Catriona Mellor, and Lise van Susteren, 'Young people's voices on climate anxiety, government betrayal and moral injury: A global phenomenon', https://papers.ssrn.com/sol3/papers.cfm?abstract_id=3918955%20
14 www.pewresearch.org/politics/2020/02/13/as-economic-concerns-recede-environmental-protection-rises-on-the-publics-policy-agenda/
15 We can think, in this regard, about the Newfoundland Regiment that saw only 68 out of 780 men answer roll call the day after the first day of the Battle of the Somme in 1916 and the famous Montreal Black Watch regiment that lost 315 of its 325 members in 1944 during the Battle of Verrières Ridge in Normandy.
16 Fletcher, Bastedo, and Hove, 2009, 911–937.

2 The Passage from a Lockean to a Hobbesian World

There is something very different about claiming the moral superiority of a liberal system based on rejection of a different ideology, as opposed to differentiating it from rogue or failed states' barbarianism and lack of respect for basic human rights. These two distinctive manners entail two irreconcilable ways of thinking about the organisation of politics and the dynamic between rulers and citizens, with the latter being inherently favourable to the implementation of liberticidal measures. This is what this chapter will explore, specifically by discussing more at length the Cold War 'liberalism of fear' compared to its post-1991 variant. I will label the former the 'Lockean paradigm' and the latter the 'Hobbesian paradigm'. What I wish to highlight in the following pages is how a Lockean view of liberalism implies the strict limitation of state powers, constant surveillance of those in charge, and citizens' willingness to make personal sacrifices, whereas a Hobbesian society is determined by the opposite reality characterised by a hierarchical and paternalist relationship between statesmen and people and by an impoverished public sphere where the protection of life takes precedence over any other considerations.

Liberalism is about allowing people to equally and freely enjoy their natural rights insofar as their actions will not impede on other people's personal freedom. As such, the state's limitation of people's negative liberty (as individual rights are usually called) will be legitimate as long as they are deemed reasonable in a free and democratic society, namely for the sake of public safety, preventing

DOI: 10.4324/9781003387749-3

disorder and crimes, for the protection of public health, and to protect the rights and freedoms of others. Tolerance of other people's behaviours is therefore the key point for understanding this ideology. According to Skhlar's aforementioned concept of the 'liberalism of fear', these are its main theoretical pillars and, as such, it is an ideology opposed to any other forms of collective life valuing opposite principles that ought, under the liberal lens, to be considered as cruel and as depriving humans of their inherent dignity. As previously mentioned, understanding liberalism as the ultimate primary good lies on conceptualisation of the fear that its benefits may be lost at any moment, which is why it requires, as a condition, an enemy who is the personification of the ultimate evil and will act as a clear and present threat to what it stands for through the deliberate imposition of physical or emotional suffering on a weaker person or group for the simple goal of achieving a political objective. Fascism and communism served as mirrors of what liberal societies had to fight against. The presence of these 'significant others' provided explicit markers to assess the value of institutional violence through understanding that some restrictions on freedom are reasonable (the minimal condition without which the exercise of freedom is impossible), as well as understanding which ones would be unjustified and could create a potentially slippery slope that may ultimately lead to arbitrary or unnecessary infringement on people's freedom.

In essence, this interpretation is very much aligned with the one John Locke proposed in his *Two Treatises on Government* and in his *Letter Concerning Toleration*; it calls on a very specific way of organising societies, with the first aspect being the importance of creating a proper institutional and constitutional framework that will prevent any domination of the majority over the minority and any potential excesses of power wielded by those who have been granted the privilege of making collective decisions in the name of the sovereign people. The Lockean view on the preservation of freedom therefore calls on the need to create and maintain deep pluralism that will allow every person and group to have a say in the decision-making process, but this should be alongside a profound distrust towards all state representatives, who are considered potential usurpers of power.

Locke famously stated that 'Wherever law ends, tyranny begins' (2003, §202). As a consequence, to prevent one individual or a group of individuals from using the tools of political power to serve their own private interests at the expense of the common good (noting that human frailty means that people will always be tempted to do so), Locke emphasises numerous times in his *Two Treatises* the importance of dividing power to prevent those in charge of making the laws from implementing them as well (2003, §143). Through this mechanism that often comes with a complex system of powers and counter-powers, it is believed that the inherently selfish interests of statesmen will inevitably be channelled into the promotion of the public good. This logic bears on the second element, namely the need for citizens to constantly keep an eye on those in charge of making decisions in the name of the people. Indeed, those who enjoy citizens' confidence are able to enjoy that trust insofar as they are not neglecting their task or infringing on people's natural rights without their consent.[1] This implies, however, that citizens should never blindly trust these individuals and that they should instead constantly keep an eye on their actions. On the contrary, though it may sound paradoxical, what liberalism requires in a large political environment where democracy can only be implemented through representation is to make the existence of trust dependent on institutionalised distrust. Indeed, genuine trust can only be experienced on a small and personal basis thanks to past experiences with individuals who have or have not disappointed us. However, in large societies, we often have to trust individuals who are completely unknown to us, such as lawyers, physicians, bus drivers, airplane pilots, and so forth. This is possible because their career and freedom depend on them acting in a way that will not be detrimental to our interests; otherwise, they know that their lack of care for other people's interests would lead them to be punished. In this sense, and similar to the need to impose basic and reasonable restrictions on people's freedom, this type of fear is justified and necessary to ensure social trust in the context of today's numerous and largely anonymous political associations. The same logic applies to the numerous counter-powers that ought to exist in liberal democracies aimed at forcing selfish individuals to act in accordance with the common good. These measures are only effective insofar as individuals are willing to sanction those who have been caught breaking the rules by removing them from office. When they are not willing to do so, tolerating a small breach of trust for the sake of avoiding political troubles will inevitably lead to greater violence and rapine. From this perspective, the survival of liberalism lies upon a dynamic of silent defiance and distrust between citizens and those in charge of making decisions in their name, and the former must fear that the latter might go rogue. This fear must be expressed in the public realm as a condition to let statesmen and other public servants know that the trust with which they have been vested is conditional upon them acting in accordance with the will of the people. In other words, in such a relationship, the citizens decide and their representatives execute their wishes.

This view of the need for an active and defiant citizenry, not as an end in itself but rather as a necessary condition to preserve one's freedom, has remained a central idea within liberal circles, such as in the works of Benjamin Constant and Alexis de Tocqueville. Comparing the citizenry–statesmen relationship to the one between rich individuals and their employees, Constant argued that not keeping an eye on how those in charge of our interests are behaving would be an idiotic attitude,[2] and de Tocqueville issued a similar warning, stating that caring exclusively about private matters entails the risk of creating a form of despotism (a mild one perhaps, but one that still endangers people's freedom).[3] Furthermore, as argued in Chapter 1, the perception of active participation as a condition for the survival of citizens' natural rights is not inimical to the idea of accepting the necessity of making personal sacrifices, even at the risk of death. On the contrary, as Patrick Henry famously said, a life deprived of freedom is not worth living (this is what he meant when he said 'Is life so dear, or peace so sweet, as to be purchased at the price of chains and slavery? Forbid it, Almighty God! I know not what course others may take; but as for me, give me liberty, or give me death!'). Such civic involvement on the part of citizens and their defiance of those in charge of managing the common good are only possible, however, when citizens are moved by the fear of experiencing tyranny and cruel treatment and when that fear supersedes any other considerations. Seeing superior value in the defence of a political principle thought to be pivotal – as was the case prior to the Cold War, with the Nazis, as well as with communism, from 1945 until 1991, regarding the importance of freedom and of opposing tyranny – has therefore managed to keep in check the predominance of biological life as people's main preoccupation and protection as states' main political obligation.

This resembles, in a way, the spirit of sacrifice the Greeks showed, which Pericles celebrated in his funeral oration. Of course, by honouring the death of a warrior who had fallen for the city, Pericles meant to celebrate the ultimate meaning of the 'good life', that is, the glorious citizen whose life was entirely dedicated to the common good. This way of thinking obviously led the Greeks to elevate the ideal of sacrifice to its purest level by associating it with the highest virtue, which Aristotle described as any action not pursued for one's own interest but rather those that are done primarily for one's country and for the sake of others (2007, 1366b) – in this case, the preservation of Athens' way of life and its collective freedom. In other words, Pericles assumed in his speech that those who had died had no other life than their political existence and that there is no life (worthy of being experienced) without politics. As such, this is not really what the Lockean logic of sacrifice refers to, as it is anchored in a more selfish desire to risk one's life not for others but rather to preserve one's own personal freedom in accordance with Locke's individualistic view of the world. However, despite this major difference from a theoretical perspective that cannot be denied, it is, nonetheless, hard to imagine, as Yvon Garlan (1974, p. 70) argued, that Athenian citizens' warrior ethos was not strongly motivated by their own personal desire to remain free from servitude or enslavement (which was, at the time, a risk associated with losing a war). From this perspective, it may be inadequate to conflate the official rhetoric of Pericles' *épitaphioi* with what might have been the prime motivation of the citizen-soldier, with the result that the latter may have actually shared more in common with the Lockean view of sacrifice.

The Hobbesian view of society is, for its, part completely different from the Lockean one. As indicated by its name, this view derives from Thomas Hobbes' philosophy and interpretation of why men agree to depart from the state of nature and unite socially and politically within a commonwealth. Hobbes imagined humanity without government, laws, or any organised society and called that 'the state of nature'. Given humans' selfish nature, the state of nature is a state of constant fear, where every person is a wolf to other people, in the sense that everyone has an equal right[4] to harm others for the sake of remaining alive, and where industry and property cannot exist. Through an obvious law of reason, humans will universally realise that this hostile reality in which they all live in 'continual fear and [in] danger of [a] violent death' and where their lives are 'poor, nasty, brutish, and short' (1994, p. 74, chap. 13) is inhospitable to their most basic concern, that is, to remain alive for as long as possible. It is this conclusion that will lead them to entrust their security to a powerful government, which Hobbes called the Leviathan. For Hobbes, because a return to the state of nature would be a calamity, the 'safety of the people (meaning their lives and property), to which he is obliged by the law of nature' (1994, p. 219, chap. 30) is accordingly the prime responsibility of this political authority.

This logic is therefore indifferent to individual freedom and rather restricts the goal of political associations to a basic objective, namely the preservation of life at all costs[5] as the underlying reason for the creation of civil society and the only belief that can unite and drive human beings in a common direction despite their having different conceptions of the good life. The fear of death, which he described as 'the greatest evil that can happen in this life' (1994, p. 219, chap. 30), rather than the fear of being deprived of one's natural rights and of being exposed as a result to cruel and inhumane treatment (as is the case with Locke), then becomes the political centrepiece of common life. This priority leads to a complete shift in the dynamic between the state and its people. If, in the Lockean view, individuals are expected to defy those ruling them, then in Hobbesian logic, they are conversely expected to be fully obedient.[6] As he wrote in *Leviathan*, people's capacity to remain safe from any danger and, as a consequence, to be prosperous depends entirely upon their obedience, which must be total (1994, p. 222, chap. 30). It is, in fact, the first commandment the sovereign ought to enforce, according to Hobbes. However, to achieve this, the state cannot rely on unilateral imposition of rules. To prevent the people's possible dissidence, close collaboration between rulers and the people is required that can only be achieved through the education of the latter regarding the reasons they need to experience a certain fear. Indeed, compliance is far easier to enforce when it does not derive from a diktat (because disobedience is always a threat) but rather from what individuals will perceive as the result of common reasoning, discussion, and thinking involving themselves and the state, where the latter takes the time to explain why the former need to fear a certain thing and why the latter needs to act. In other words, the simple fear of being punished is not sufficient here, and for the laws to be respected, individuals must be convinced that it is in their best interest to abide by them. More precisely, this synergy implies concord between citizens and the state in a way where the latter will be perceived by the former as simply responding to their wishes – a desire that is, in fact, the result of an acculturation process that the state has actually achieved through its co-optation of other actors who will instil into people from a very young age the necessity of following a certain course of action, this course of action being to refrain from behaving in a way that will threaten other individuals' lives. From this perspective, the source of fear in a Hobbesian society is therefore not the sole result of a prince or a Leviathan imposing their will on the people but instead the outcome of a more insidious collaborative form of oppression that includes all actors of society.[7] 'Educating the people' is therefore a core duty of the sovereign authority that can take many forms, that is, either through the school system or through co-optation of the legacy media entrusted with the diffusion of a certain message of fear that favours the government's concentration of powers – a feat that has become increasingly easy given the growing financial dependency of legacy media on the state because of new digital technologies.[8] When this is the case, obedience to state authorities becomes almost second nature, and people will naturally obey the rules, not because of the fear of being punished for not respecting them but rather out of their own conscience that has been shaped accordingly. When such a process has been perfected, it is individuals themselves that will ask the state authorities to impose restrictions on their own freedom, the preservation of which will become secondary and subordinated to the necessity of remaining alive. For the reasons I have already elucidated, this is hardly conceivable in a world where the dominant fear is value-based and where a Lockean view of the world prevails, as people will be more wary of any action that may infringe on their personal freedom.

The Hobbesian logic therefore has a lot to do with what Michel Foucault (2004) called 'governmentality', namely the science of how to pacify and control individuals for the sake of guaranteeing peace and safety by disciplining them. For Foucault, this need to domesticate people and restrict their freedom was a necessity following the collapse of religious beliefs at the time of modernity.[9] If, during the medieval period, religion acted as a beacon of moral behaviours, the nascent atheism of the Renaissance created the need to find new answers to the question 'How should I behave?'. As exemplified in the works of Machiavelli and Hobbes, the state simply took over the role of conducting people's souls, which the French philosopher Marcel Gauchet labelled as the political sphere's reappropriation of the theological matrix. The answer to the abovementioned question was the need to live in peace, which is why the notion of the 'reason of state' unsurprisingly emerged in the same period. This concept that finds its roots in Machiavelli and Hobbes' time emancipated itself from ancient ethics and religion by developing its own unique ratio that sees ensuring social peace and the safety of the people as the sole goals of politics, even if it implies resorting to immoral actions. Associated with the idea of 'state crime', this reason must be understood as an amoral reality that can justify violence whenever necessity is called upon to prevent societies from falling into an anarchic state of nature that would inevitably lead to people's death. The fear of sedition and strategies to prevent it constituted the primary concern of authors of that time, such as Francis Bacon, Giovanni Botero, and Giovanni Palazzo, who devoted their time to assessing the reasons leading to the development of these sorts of troubles and who also pondered the most efficient ways to resolve them.

Although Hobbes is hailed as a liberal philosopher for his concept of the social contract and his idea of equality among people, we must realise that the theory he came up with is not inherently linked with that ideology. On the contrary, it is rather a theory of social control that is bounded by no limits as long as people believe that the restrictions they are being asked to follow are reasonable. This is nothing less than a slippery slope when we acknowledge that individuals can, with very little effort, be quite easily convinced to be wary of a specific threat. Consequently, unlike Locke's philosophy, there is nothing that can prevent the Hobbesian perspective on the role of the state evolving from an individual rights-friendly position to one that recognises no objection to limiting these rights for the sake of people's safety. The 9/11 terrorist attacks, the ongoing climate change crisis, and the COVID-19 pandemic are good examples in this regard. Indeed, Al-Qaeda's terrorist attack on that fateful morning of September

11, 2001, has literally forever changed the lives of people in the United States (and the West). As *The New York Times* columnist David Brooks (2019) wrote, in an instant, everything changed. Since then, the news has been filled with horror stories of people being beheaded, women being stoned, and people receiving envelopes filled with anthrax-like white powder, even though the actual risk of being killed by a foreign terrorist was at the time and is still today lower than the probability of dying from choking on a piece of food.[10] However, far from leading to the development of a renewed willingness to fight for what Western liberal societies stand for, as was the case during the Cold War, this threat conversely favoured cowardice and hysteria over any bag left unattended in a public place or even a water bottle inadvertently left in a backpack at airport security. This hysterical fear had a snowball effect on other so-called dangers such as the 2014–2016 Ebola outbreak in Africa that led people to wear hazmat suits in public and withdraw their children from school because an employee had recently travelled to a(n) (unaffected) country in the region (Brooks, 2014). Unsurprisingly, the COVID-19 pandemic created the same frenzy.

When it comes to the COVID-19 pandemic, as briefly argued in the Introduction, although the virus proved to be deadly, its lethality was, in fact, largely restricted to very specific group of individuals, primarily the elderly[11] and those already suffering from medical preconditions, such as obesity, immunodeficiencies, chronic lung diseases, and Down syndrome. Even if such individuals have been more susceptible to dying as a result of COVID-19, the fatality rate has remained low, which is why the overall percentage of infected individuals who died due to the virus is very similar to the figures for twentieth-century pandemics (apart from the Spanish flu). In light of this, were all the Chinese-like liberticidal measures imposed on us to prevent the spread of this virus justified? They obviously would be in a Hobbesian society in which every life matters and protecting people's lives is thought to be the state's main responsibility. From such a perspective, implemented measures are very often exaggerated and disproportionate to the threat individuals are actually facing. In this case, a proportionate reaction would have been to focus on the places where individuals who are more susceptible to dying due to the virus are concentrated, such as nursing homes and hospitals. This could have been achieved by requiring visitors and employees to wear a mask or show a recent PCR test with a negative result. All other measures imposed on able-bodied individuals were simply disproportionate (or useless)[12] with regard to the threat they were actually facing. However, in a world where avoiding death (even when the chances of succumbing to it are slim to none) is paramount, no measure is deemed too extreme.

Furthermore, this pandemic has contributed to demonstrating what I previously described, namely the need for a Hobbesian state to ensure that the people do not oppose liberticidal measures but rather welcome them with open arms. When this is the case, a spirit of balance that acknowledges that the need to act, when facing a specific challenge, in a way that will be the least detrimental possible in terms of infringement on people's individual freedom simply cannot exist; the power of irrational fear will simply prevail over any other considerations, and nothing will stop the state from imposing uselessly harmful measures on people who will, far from criticising them, actually embrace them. Indeed, what has been amazing throughout this pandemic is the fact that a significant majority of people were not only fine with the measures imposed on them but were also open to additional ones. For instance, mask wearing still proved to be highly popular in Canada weeks after the official mandatory mask-wearing mandate had been abandoned, and 69% of Canadians said, according to a November 2022 poll, that they would either totally support (52%) or somewhat support (17%) the reinstatement of this policy.[13] In France, 76% of people polled in December 2022 said that they would favour the reintroduction of the mask mandate on public transport and 58% said they would favour the same in all public places. Further, 66% of respondents said they were concerned about the then-upcoming Christmas holidays, and half of them expressed the intention to either observe social distancing or avoid gatherings as much as possible.[14] The polarising question of mandatory vaccination has also shown how the fear of death has taken over in Western societies and how people – an overwhelming majority of whom are not susceptible to dying from COVID-19 – have shown little interest in honouring other people's freedom of choice despite the fact that the vaccine manufacturers clearly stated that the vaccine does not prevent transmission or contraction of the virus. In Canada, there was, in fact, no real debate on this topic as the majority of people showed great support for mandatory vaccination.[15] In France,

68% of people were favourable towards this idea as of November 2021,[16] which was an increase from a few months prior (58% in July).[17] Even measures objectively irrelevant in terms of stopping viral spread, such as a night-time curfew (as if the virus was not circulating during the day), which was imposed in January 2021 in Quebec, garnered massive support (74%).[18] Additionally, we also ought to mention that unvaccinated individuals were denied organ transplants in some jurisdictions,[19] and some parents lost custody of their children.[20] Furthermore, as I have stated earlier, a Hobbesian state cannot function without the support of its people, who must collaborate by understanding that the restrictions the statesmen want to impose are necessary for the populace's well-being. As a result, the people themselves can end up becoming the most tyrannical and liberticidal entities when they are truly convinced of the nature of a threat they are told the state is facing. The pandemic has been a textbook example of this, with numerous individuals urging the state to impose completely disproportional measures against the unvaccinated, like disallowing them from leaving home or having a job,[21] or even incarcerating them, as numerous polls have shown,[22] and denying them medical treatment[23] (or forcing them to pay for it out of pocket).[24] Lastly, in the Spring of 2020, it was reported that nearly 70% of phone calls the police were receiving comprised individuals denouncing their neighbours or acquaintances for not respecting the lockdown rules,[25] an action that many public officials[26] and celebrities[27] encouraged.

This intolerance of the dissidence of a few is understandable in a Hobbesian world where individuals are expected to integrate into their psyche the need to act in a way that will not be detrimental to other people's lives. As Hobbes wrote, the notion that people ought to be left to think on their own regarding what is a good or wrong action ought to be fought as a seditious idea that can only weaken the state's authority and its capacity to act. As such, those favouring the expression of a diversity of private consciousnesses that contradict the state's doxa can only cause trouble; Hobbes equated such persons to proponents of 'false doctrines' and 'little worms' who must be silenced (1994, p. 218, chap. 29). This view, written almost 400 years ago, bears a lot of similarity with how those who were criticising the measures imposed during the pandemic were treated, that is, as dangerous individuals supporting 'fake news' and propagators of misinformation who had to be criminalised and treated as quasi-enemies of the state (and certainly not as decent citizens). This fanaticism towards those not abiding by the dominant viewpoint is further reinforced in a situation where the *homo superstes* conception of life prevails, since what needs to be preserved, that is, life itself, is non-negotiable and not something we can compromise on as each of us only has one life to experience. The same intolerance does not exist to such an extent in a Lockean perspective, where the manner with which liberal societies ought to fight against an ideological enemy is more open to discussion and dissidence, since its risk of overtaking us is (outside of periods of intense political crisis) largely theoretical. From this perspective, criticising and opposing the state for its actions does not lead, in the general mind of the people, to the same detrimental consequences for the dissenters, which may explain why the danger of communism and strategies to overcome it were, during most of the Cold War, assessed in a diverse manner in Western societies (with many people even embracing this ideology). This is, however, inconceivable when it is largely believed that death can strike against anyone at any time.

It is fairly easy to understand this dynamic between citizens who abide by the dominant logic and those who question it. In accordance with Hobbes' view on the state's most important function, that is, to keep people's behaviour in line with their own safety and that of others, anyone who puts a higher value on principles other than the protection of life can only be perceived as a dangerous threat. As such, the pandemic has allowed us to witness a clash between the Lockean and the Hobbesian views of society and how deeply incompatible they are with one another. When the Hobbesian viewpoint prevails, individuals seem to forget about the value of individual rights and freedom – a tendency that seems more present in Western societies than in countries where the people still have a vivid memory of totalitarianism (e.g. in the former Soviet republics and in Eastern Europe) and, accordingly, appear to be more prudent than their Western counterparts regarding trusting their government, knowing the price that could ultimately result from doing so. There are, of course, many reasons (some of them cultural and economic) that can explain people's defiance of their state, as I have already explained elsewhere (Caron, 2022b; Caron & Thibault, 2022), but it is difficult to ignore that Lockean logic may have played a significant role as well. The way Western analysts have perceived this factor is also symptomatic of how their views of liberalism have shifted away from Locke's perspective and towards a Hobbesian one. Indeed, the lack of trust in these societies has been attributed to the fact that democracy is still very young compared to Western Europe or America (Furlong, 2021), assuming that this regime requires citizens' confidence in their state. Although this may be the case under a Hobbesian perspective, it is far from being so under a Lockean one, where people are expected to question and survey political authority. For people who have lived in servitude at a time in their life and who can still testify about the horrors of totalitarianism to their children and grandchildren, resisting is perceived as a healthy behaviour to have in a democracy, whether it is nascent or old. Of course, when one's mind has shifted to the Hobbesian viewpoint, this idea seems odd and even dangerous, which is not surprising considering the degree of incompatibility between these two views of society.

Furthermore, when a Hobbesian conception of life takes over, the risks of seeing governmental abuses are huge, as government actors will usually extend the use of the tools granted to them to other aspects of our lives. However, since citizens' initial decision to participate in fashioning such tools would have been taken in a state of panic, the potential for excessive governmental use of said tools would not have been considered in the manner that they would have been considered from a Lockean perspective, out of fear of being marginalised for one's opposition. The 9/11 attacks triggered a major shift in this regard, and the Patriot Act constitutes a good example of this phenomenon. Though the Patriot Act was initially designed as short-term legislation intended to help government agencies combat terrorism, this law has since been regularly renewed and has now become a common tool at the disposal of the US government for use in cases that have nothing to do with anti-terrorist purposes. Quite unsurprisingly, the various measures imposed during the pandemic also went beyond their initial objectives, as a December 2022 Associated Press report dramatically revealed (Burke et al., 2022). As it turned out, the various data governments (democratic and authoritarian alike) had been collecting about people ostensibly 'strictly for health purposes' ended up being used for non-related reasons, such as harassing marginalised groups and activists. For instance, in Israel, hundreds of individuals who participated in the Spring 2021 Al-Aqsa clashes with Israeli security forces (or who were simply living or working nearby) received a text message reading, in Arabic: 'You have been identified as having participated in acts of violence in the Al-Aqsa Mosque. We will hold you accountable'. It is suspected that the COVID-19 tracking application people downloaded on their phones had been repurposed by the Shin Bet (Israel's security agency) for motives obviously unrelated to health reasons. A similar situation unfolded in Australia where an application requiring individuals to use a QR code before entering numerous public places (so that they could be contacted in the event of a COVID-19 outbreak) was used by law enforcement authorities to contact around 2,500 people who had been at an event where a murder happened. The problem with these sorts of technologies is that it is very difficult (if not impossible) to put the toothpaste back in the tube, and there is a high risk that these unforeseen applications of tools initially specified for a particular purpose will easily become the new normal.

If we resume contemplating states' pandemic response, we also need to wonder why they pushed so hard on the idea that the full complement of COVID-19 countermeasures had to be implemented to save as many lives as possible. It is, in fact, a natural outcome of the vicious circle created by the phenomenon described earlier, that is, making sure, through various means, that people integrate within their mindset that their sole enemy is death itself and that the state can legitimately impose measures that will allow individuals to avoid suffering such an outcome. As noted, whenever that logic becomes an integral part of people's psyche, they lose track of the red lines states should not cross at the risk of losing their liberal nature. If this is necessary for any Hobbesian state, then the state also ends up creating for itself terrible popular pressure that it needs to satisfy at the risk of triggering a schism with the people it is serving. The risk here concerns the people overtaking the state in their view of what constitutes danger. If this were to happen, the Leviathan runs the risk of being perceived by the people as an entity that is unable to protect them, which can only lead to a challenge to the state's legitimacy. Consequently, the political sphere is condemned to constantly go further in terms of offering protection. The Hobbesian state is, in other words, doomed to become, as Dr Frankenstein, the slave of its own creation by always having to satisfy its citizens' endless and ever-growing demand for protection. This Hobbesian society determined by the fear of death and by a purely biological conception of life, as we have witnessed during the COVID-19 pandemic, may very well just be the first glimpse of another danger humanity is facing, namely climate change. It seems as though a similar pattern is emerging with regard to climate change, that is, a growing trend aimed at making people accept this reality as a precondition for their ultimate acceptance of related restrictions on their lives that will seriously hinder their margin of freedom. Achieving this will be made easier by the fact that the demotion of the Lockean perspective on life in favour of the Hobbesian one has also affected social mobilisation. Indeed, as I explained in Chapter 1 with reference to a few national liberation movements, many of the Cold War mobilisations that were value-based and required personal sacrifices have slowly but surely been replaced by apocalyptic political causes. What explains this sudden awareness and call for action can only be attributed, in my view, to the Hobbesian lens through which people have gradually started to understand the meaning of human existence in the last few decades. Having lived their entire lives in a world that fears death and where everything is conditioned to facilitate the pursuit of happiness as people's inherent and natural right, people should not be surprised to see how concerned members of the younger generations are with the environmental cause, a cause that bears no similarity to any previous one. Whereas former struggles for independence or against totalitarian regimes were principle-based, the environmental movement is inherently a Hobbesian fight for survival that bears no similarity to former political causes. In this regard, Greta Thunberg and her followers cannot be compared in any way with Vaclav Havel, the Czech dissident and the last president of Czechoslovakia, nor with all those who decided to challenge communism in the Eastern Bloc during the Cold War. If the latter's sacrifices were value-based and entailed significant consequences for their lives (which were deemed unworthy of living under a dictatorship), the undertakings of the former entail no negative impacts on their existence or well-being and are solely aimed at surviving as long as possible. We can already predict the types of restrictions that apocalyptic causes will eventually lead states to impose – which will be welcomed by their people.

Already, some individuals who might be considered *avant-gardistes* have openly argued that restricting the number of times people can travel by plane within a certain period could be an option[28] as could limiting the number of farms to decrease meat consumption.[29] Although these ideas might seem far-fetched now, they are, nonetheless, indicative of the liberticidal trend gaining steam in Western societies for the sake of preserving life. This glimpse of the near future resembles an ecological 'Platonistic republic' where individuals' lives are closely supervised by a few 'just ones'.

Conclusion

Similar to a religious belief that necessitates the presence of an evil spirit that serves as a counter-example of what members of the faith stand for, ideologies – which have often been called 'secular religions' – require the same oppositional figure that will highlight their uniqueness and superiority. This is what liberalism has done by opposing itself to the things from which it was made to protect us. If, during the Cold War, the fear of communism helped individuals uphold higher moral values and principles, then the collapse of the 'Evil Empire' in 1991 has led liberalism to define itself as the only political system that can prevent individuals from dying. This shift to a *homo superstes* conception of human existence was by no mean anecdotal. Rather, it has meant a profound political change with ramifications that are only becoming obvious to many of us, thanks to the COVID-19 pandemic.

In a way, this change made possible under the 'end of history' theory may have meant, in a paradoxical way, the slow erosion of liberal values. Indeed, liberalism ought to stand for the preservation of natural rights, allowing individuals to equally enjoy their negative freedom insofar as our actions do not hinder the same capacity in others. Enjoying such a possibility is, however, very fragile, and those fortunate enough to enjoy such personal liberty ought to be wary of any attempts by external or domestic forces that would result in their servitude, which is why people must be willing to actively defend these rights against any potential usurpers. This is, in essence, what the Lockean paradigm is all about – fruition of the only genuinely liberal type of society. In such a society, fear is conducive to civic engagement, specifically the fear of being denied one's personal freedom. When individuals understand that, for humans, life is only worth living when one has the capacity to freely choose one's path, they become willing to accept the need to fight to preserve their *modus vivendi*. They know that, in comparison to servitude, death might be the better alternative. On the other hand, for the reasons that I have elucidated, Western societies have gradually moved away from this paradigm and have instead espoused a Hobbesian conception of society that places a higher value on remaining alive, with the consequence that individuals have come to terms with the idea that this objective can be pursued at the expense of their freedom – a shift that culminated in 2020–2022, with the imposition of harsh liberticidal measures in many liberal societies.

One of the main consequences of this purely biological Hobbesian conception of life is the slow development of a situation akin to social tyranny. Indeed, to guarantee the social acceptability of disproportionate restrictions on individual freedom, it is necessary for those affected by them to welcome these limitations; otherwise, they would revolt against them. As I have argued, this requires the state to create conditions that will enable it to convince people of the seriousness of the dangers they are facing. When this has been achieved, people will be willing to embrace the restrictions imposed on them and will, in turn, generate profound antagonism towards anyone refusing to abide by them. As their lives and safety will be deemed endangered because of these non-compliers, they will not hesitate to direct at them the most serious and heinous criticisms that will be so harsh (especially the threats levelled at them) so as to ultimately lead to the creation of a societal lead weight that will force the dissenters to either conform or face long-lasting social isolation. We have seen, during the COVID-19 pandemic, how fusion of the fear of dying and the display of exemplary behaviours mutually reinforced both and allowed states to easily implement – very often by decrees and without the approval of the legislative branch – liberticidal measures similar to those in force in totalitarian China, measures that would have been even more harmful to people's freedom if their severity had been up to the people themselves.

This is the practical meaning of the liberalism of fear based on a Hobbesian viewpoint. Unlike under the Lockean alternative, the differences between liberal democracies and authoritarian/totalitarian regimes are vanishing. In light of the other challenges that are emerging (e.g. climate change), there is no reason to believe that this trend will stop. On the contrary, the apocalyptic future humankind is facing according to what state officials and activists are repeating day after day, combined with the solutions societies will have to accept to survive, is opening up a perspective where the exceptionalism of the COVID-19 pandemic may be normalised. This outcome, that is, perpetually living in a state of emergency is another important element to consider when it comes to the worrisome evolution of liberal societies since the end of the Cold War. This is the subject of the analysis presented in Chapter 3.

Notes

1 He wrote:

> Though in a constituted commonwealth, standing upon its own basis, and acting according to its own nature, that is, acting for the preservation of the community, there can be but one supreme power, which is the legislative, to which all the rest are and must be subordinate; yet the legislative being only a fiduciary power to act for certain ends, there remains still 'in the people a supreme power to remove or alter the legislative', when they find the legislative act contrary to the trust reposed in them[;] for all power given with trust for attaining an end, being limited by that end[,] whenever that end is manifestly neglected or opposed, the trust must necessarily be forfeited, and the power devolve into the hands of those that gave it, who may place it anew where they shall think best for their safety and security.
>
> (2003, §149)

2 He wrote about political representation as follows:

> It is nothing but an organization by means of which a nation charges a few individuals to do what it can't or doesn't want to do itself. Poor men look after their own affairs; rich ones hire stewards. This is the story of ancient nations and modern nations. The representative system is a mandate given to a certain number of men by the mass of the people who want their interests to be defended but don't have the time to defend them constantly themselves. But, unless they are idiots, rich men who employ stewards keep a close and strict watch on whether they are doing their duty, making sure that they aren't negligent, corruptible, or incapable; and if they are prudent[,] the landowners will judge how well their mandate is being carried out by staying well-informed about the affairs the stewards have been entrusted to carry out. In the same way, the people who

resort to the representative system so as to enjoy the liberty that suits them, should exercise an active and constant surveillance over their representatives, and reserve for themselves the right – at times that aren't too far apart – to discard them if they betray their trust, and to revoke any powers they have abused.

(1988, p. 325–326)

3 See, in particular, the section of *Democracy in America* (2000) titled 'What kind of despotism democratic nations have to fear'.
4 The capacity to behave in a harmful manner towards others is shared equally among humans, according to Hobbes. He wrote that

> Nature hath made men so equal in the faculties of body and mind as that, though there be found one man sometimes manifestly stronger in body or of quicker mind than another, yet when all is reckoned together the difference between man and man is not so considerable as that one man can thereupon claim to himself any benefit to which another may not pretend as well as he. For as to the strength of body, the weakest has strength enough to kill the strongest, either by secret machination or by confederacy with others that are in the same danger with himself.

(1994, p. 74, chap. 13)

5 This led Skhlar to believe that, despite being founded on a social contract between citizens and their statesmen, Hobbes' so-called liberalism is a misleading view as it has nothing to do with the core elements of this ideology (1989, p. 24).
6 To understand Locke's view on obedience, see Chapter XIX, Section 228 of his *Two Treatises of Government*.
7 Regarding the 'common people's minds', Hobbes wrote in *Leviathan* that 'Unless they be tainted with dependence on the potent, or scribbled over with the opinions of their doctors, [they] are like clean paper, fit to receive whatsoever by public authority shall be imprinted in them' (1994, p. 221, chap. 30).
8 State-provided financial aid to legacy media reached about 600 million euros per year in France, and in 2019, Germany announced the inaugural provision of such support, which totalled 40 million euros for 2020 and later reached 200 million euros. During the COVID-19 pandemic, this aid has also increased significantly. www.lesechos.fr/tech-medias/medias/coronavirus-le-gouvernement-a-debloque-2-milliards-pour-les-medias-1221356. In Quebec, where financial support for legacy media is also very significant (at 50 million dollars per year), the government has announced that it will no longer buy advertisements in media that do not fully support its measures.

9 It is interesting to note the direct influence of this pattern on Hobbes' *Leviathan*. At a time when the notion of a monarch ruling by divine right was being challenged, his goal was to find new foundations for absolutism that were not grounded in religious beliefs.
10 www.nbcnews.com/news/us-news/you-re-more-likely-die-choking-be-killed-foreign-terrorists-n715141. It was, in fact, estimated in 2011, that the chance of a British person being murdered in a terrorist attack was 1 in 63,280,444. See www.cato.org/blog/chance-being-murdered-or-injured-terrorist-attack-united-kingdom
11 In Canada, from March 2020 until mid-May 2021, 93% of the deaths attributed to COVID-19 were among people aged 65 years and over. (www150.statcan.gc.ca/n1/pub/75-006-x/2021001/article/00008-eng.htm). See also Hoffmann and Wolf (2021).
12 It is important to note that, despite the large-scale use of lockdowns, their efficiency has been largely debated and more and more studies are indicating, thanks to the perspective we now have, that these efforts amounted to almost nothing, namely a 3.2% reduction in deaths on average, at the most (Fraser Institute, 2023). Although this is not insignificant, this number must, nonetheless, be compared with the other costs of lockdowns, such as increased incidence of domestic violence and drug-, alcohol-, and mental health-related issues, as well as employment disruptions. However, in terms of lives saved, we should not ignore that lockdowns also led to an increase in deaths. The Fraser Institute (2023) stated that

> Behaviour changes in the face of COVID-19 and lockdowns included forms of self-protection that often ended up increasing mortality. These behaviour changes included missing regular medical checkups out of fear of contracting the disease. Estimates in the US show that there were 171,000 excess non-COVID-19 deaths through to the end of 2021. By that time, the US had recorded 825,929 COVID-19 deaths. However, if lockdowns only reduce deaths by 3.2 percent, then only 27,303 lives were saved by lockdowns. Just on collateral deaths alone the cost/benefit ratio of lockdown is 171,000/27,303 = 6.26.

13 www.ctvnews.ca/health/coronavirus/majority-of-canadians-support-return-of-face-masks-in-indoor-public-spaces-if-deemed-necessary-survey-1.6144419
14 www.lefigaro.fr/sciences/les-francais-favorables-au-retour-du-masque-obligatoire-dans-l-espace-public-20221211
15 https://globalnews.ca/news/8124103/canada-election-mandatory-vaccines-Covid-poll/
16 www.lejdd.fr/Societe/sondage-Covid-19-68-des-francais-sont-favorables-a-la-vaccination-obligatoire-4078839

The Passage from a Lockean to a Hobbesian World   67

17 www.francetvinfo.fr/sante/maladie/coronavirus/vaccin/Covid-19-les-francais-majoritairement-favorables-a-la-vaccination-obligatoire-selon-notre-sondage_4686011.html
18 www.lesaffaires.com/dossier/Covid-19-tout-ce-qu-il-faut-savoir/une-majorite-de-quebecois-appuie-le-couvre-feu-selon-un-sondage/622494
19 www.cbc.ca/news/canada/edmonton/appeal-court-rejects-unvaccinated-woman-s-request-to-get-back-on-transplant-list-1.6644849
20 www.usatoday.com/story/news/world/2022/02/06/unvaccinated-dad-loses-custody-children/6684144001/; www.latimes.com/california/story/2022-01-06/Covid-19-vaccinations-family-court
21 As was the case with American actor Sean Penn. www.dailywire.com/news/sean-penn-says-being-unvaccinated-is-criminal-and-those-people-shouldnt-leave-their-homes
22 Back in January 2022, 27% of Canadians reportedly favoured such a measure. www.nsnews.com/coronavirus-Covid-19-local-news/study-finds-that-27-of-canadians-support-jail-time-for-the-unvaccinated-4975408
23 www.theatlantic.com/health/archive/2022/01/unvaccinated-medical-care-hospitals-omicron/621299/
24 www.capital.fr/economie-politique/les-francais-sont-ils-daccord-pour-faire-payer-aux-non-vaccines-leurs-frais-dhospitalisation-1425036
25 www.francetvinfo.fr/sante/maladie/coronavirus/confinement-la-delation-represente-jusqu-a-70-des-appels-dans-certaines-grandes-agglomerations-selon-le-syndicat-alternative-police_3914689.html; www.reuters.com/article/us-health-coronavirus-germany-denunciati-idUSKBN21K2PB
26 www.lapresse.ca/actualites/Covid-19/2020-12-17/denoncer-les-partys-de-noel-c-est-la-chose-a-faire-dit-plante.php
27 www.cliqueduplateau.com/2020/05/27/guy-a-lepage-et-rachid-badouri-sont-des-stools/
28 www.lexpress.fr/environnement/trois-a-quatre-vols-sur-toute-une-vie-le-pdg-de-voyageurs-du-monde-repond-a-jancovici_2184426.html
29 www.magjournal77.fr/politique-et-societe/item/56486-rechauffement-climatique-les-vaches-polluent-et-la-deputee-sandrine-rousseau-veut-agir

3 State of Emergency or a New Governance Paradigm

The *homo superstes* conception of human existence that Western societies have been witnessing over the past 30 years has not only shifted people's understanding of what they ought to fear, the relationship they ought to have with their state, and the value of personal sacrifices but also of the extent of what is considered to be legitimate state action. In concrete terms, this means that for anything considered to be a life-threatening menace, there is a growing tendency to perceive it as requiring exceptional measures only, with the direct consequences of banalising risk and marginalising legislative powers in favour of reinforcing the executive branch. In other words, the *homo superstes* conception of life is intimately connected with a new paradigm of governance that sees the superiority of 'deciding' over 'deliberating' with regard to a growing number of so-called exceptional threats thought to be unsolvable through the normal judicial tools of the state – a situation that gives full meaning to Albert Camus' warning in *The Plague* that no one can ever be free in a world constantly at the mercy of scourges and pestilences. Consequently, this logic tends to move liberal societies in a direction where it is becoming increasingly acceptable and justified for statesmen to suspend or hinder individuals' freedom, a view that can only erode the very meaning of liberalism that we owe to Locke's philosophy.

According to Abraham Lincoln's famous Gettysburg address, individual freedom can only be guaranteed when there is a 'government of the people, by the people and for the people'. Indeed, looking at dictatorships around the world, it is clear that the

DOI: 10.4324/9781003387749-4

State of Emergency or a New Governance Paradigm 69

hijacking of power by a minority of individuals for whatever purpose has systematically led to the erosion of people's individual liberty and their transformation from citizens into mere subjects. It is for this reason that all decisions impacting people's lives have to be made either by themselves through direct democracy or through individuals who are elected to make decisions in their name, which is called representative democracy. In the representative system, elected individuals become members of the legislative branch, and it is expected that they will be held accountable for all their decisions. As I have argued in the previous pages, despite the fact that these representatives are 'entrusted' by the people with the duty of making decisions for the common wellbeing, this expression is, nonetheless, profoundly misleading. Indeed, the people's trust is not a blind one but rather an outcome of the relationship of distrust they will maintain with their representatives. In other words, the confidence that people can have in their representatives' willingness to act in accordance with their well-being will be the result of the citizenry keeping constant watch over the actions and decisions of the members of the legislative branch, where said decisions should always follow thorough and public deliberations. If people were to neglect this necessary duty of surveillance, there would be a high risk of their representatives privileging their private interests and gradually diminishing people's freedom. To prevent that evil outcome, it is also thought to be necessary to divide powers as much as possible, so that one potential abuse of power would end up having only limited consequences on people's lives (Friedrich, 1937). Hence, democracy is a much slower political system than any other type of regime when it comes to the decision-making process, but this disadvantage is seen as necessary for the sake of preserving people's freedom.

However, there are extraordinary and exceptional situations where deliberation can be an unwanted constraint that could paradoxically end up harming people's freedom. When societies are exposed to such extreme situations, the aforementioned mechanisms may have to be disabled in favour of concentrating power in the hands of one individual or a single institutional body. This is a well-known dilemma of liberal governments, that is, accepting that the system that normally allows individual rights and personal freedom to be protected can sometimes prevent the government from responding efficiently to a situation so serious that it threatens these very principles.[1] Even John Locke agreed that these states of emergencies justified what he called 'executive prerogative', that is, allowing the executive branch to exercise full power for the sake of the common good.[2] However, the author of *Two Treatises on Government* was not proposing anything original in this regard, as his proposition was largely modelled upon the ancient institution of Roman dictatorship that had been called 'perhaps the most strikingly successful of all known systems of emergency government' (Watkins, 1940, p. 332) and was a system primarily designed for 'getting things done' (*dictatura rei gerundae causa*) and 'suppressing civil insurrection' (*dictatura seditionis sedandae causa*). If the latter function was activated when there was a threat of civil war, where one party was threatening to take power in the republic, the former was used to prevent the republic from military defeat at the hands of an enemy. In any of these cases, the normal institutional practices of the Roman Republic were suspended, and one individual (the dictator) was given kingship powers for a maximum period of six months to solve the specific crisis he had been appointed to address. It goes without saying that appointing a dictator with such immense powers came with a huge risk for the republic, namely that the individual would refuse to hand over his prerogatives to the Senate and to the people of Rome once his mission had been accomplished. This risk was, however, minimised by the fact that the Romans were keen on choosing a highly virtuous individual who had already shown his dedication to the values of the republic. In this regard, the most discussed example is Quinctius Cincinnatus who, while ploughing his field, famously received a request from the Senate to act as a dictator in order to save Rome from a foreign invasion, a mission he accepted and fulfilled in only 16 days, after which he returned to his farm.[3]

Perceived as a necessary component of any democracy, some modern liberal states have transparently included in their constitution a similar provision aimed at temporarily increasing the powers of the head of state/government (depending on the presidential vs. parliamentary nature of the regime, respectively) to make them more reactive in times of emergencies. This executive prerogative has even been used in the recent past. This was notoriously the case in France in 1961 when then President Charles de Gaulle used the powers of Article 16 of the constitution for five months after a short-lived military putsch in Algiers openly threatened to overthrow the republican order. However, de Gaulle had already used this method three years before – albeit unofficially, since it was not enshrined at the time in what was then the constitution of the Fourth Republic. Indeed, following the creation of a public safety committee (*Comité de salut public*) by a military junta in Algeria that later took control of the island of Corsica before threatening to take control of Paris via a combined airborne assault and the use of armoured units, de Gaulle was named *président du Conseil* (the equivalent of prime minister) by then President René Coty but only after he had made his decision conditional on the National Assembly granting him full powers for six months, during which he prepared for the transition to a new constitutional order (the Fifth Republic, under which France is still operating) that was ultimately approved by a nationwide referendum.

Although the logic is similar to that of the Roman dictatorship, the contemporary model of emergency powers bears a significant difference compared to the former. If, in the case of Rome, full powers were granted to a virtuous individual whose *fides* was beyond any doubt, the current model instead de facto entrusts that power to the holder of a position (head of government/head of state) without knowing in advance the personal identity of who may wield it.[4] In other words, what Carl Friedrich perceived as one of the strengths of Roman dictatorship, that is, the clear-cut separation between the institution entitled to declare the state of emergency and the individual in charge of emergency powers, has now disappeared in modern constitutions (1937, p. 211), which basically allow an unvirtuous individual to abuse emergency powers after having been elected to a position that enables said person to directly or indirectly trigger exceptional mechanisms, as was the case with Hitler in 1933[5] and with Indira Gandhi in India from 1975 until 1977. Under these circumstances, a tool designed to save democracy in emergency situations can therefore easily lead to its complete disappearance and replacement by an authoritarian state.

Apart from these few cases, the potential for abuse may explain why the state of exception in the twentieth century followed the British model that does not confer authority on any institutions before it has been granted by an act of Parliament (contrary to

Article 16 of the French constitution which references an act of the executive),[6] thereby ensuring, following a typical Lockean perspective, that the legislative branch (and, henceforth, the people) remains in full control of deciding when to initiate such an exceptional departure from the constitutional order and also makes decisions concerning monitoring its use and deciding whether to extend or suspend its application. Furthermore, more in line with its own self-understanding in an era of authoritarian rule, this view that we can label as the 'legislative model', which acquires its legitimacy from the people (at least indirectly through the legislative branch), is another brick in the structure of the liberalism of fear that sees itself as being antithetical to a strong and omnipotent executive more akin to repressive and illiberal governments.

However, not only does this control remain largely theoretical, but this state of emergency model has also paradoxically contributed to the enlargement of executive branch prerogatives and has also led to the establishment of permanent changes in the legal system.[7] The war against terror following the 9/11 attacks and the COVID-19 pandemic have both revealed this shift and its liberticidal consequences in people's lives. States indeed have at their disposal at the legislative level measures to face emergencies without having to openly suspend the constitutional order. This is, for example, the case with France's 1955 State of Emergency Act (*Loi relative à l'état d'urgence*) that allows the government to impose exceptional measures when the country is under grave and immediate threat. Thus far, it has been used during the Algerian crisis, in New Caledonia in 1984–1985, in Wallis and Futuna in 1986, in French Polynesia in 1987, in 2005 following the riots in the country's suburbs, and from 2015 to 2017 after France suffered various terrorist attacks. Initially adopted as a way to face the troubles in Algeria, this law has since undergone a major evolution that has gradually led to the marginalisation of legislative power. Adopted at a time of the Fourth Republic when the powers of the French presidency were mostly ceremonial, its implementation depended solely upon the wishes of the National Assembly until 1960 when it became the prerogative of the executive branch. However, the implementation of these powers cannot exceed 12 days without the Assembly's approval.

As it is often said, the devil is in the details, and if we turn our attention to the way this law was used from 2015 to 2017 to face

State of Emergency or a New Governance Paradigm 73

the terrorist threat, we can clearly see how problematic the legislative model of emergency powers can be, given that it has allowed the authorities to, among other things, prevent individuals from participating in public protests, impose house arrest, and extend the duration for which they can hold individuals suspected of terrorism in custody. Firstly, we need to mention the circumstances under which the law was adopted. Indeed, even though former French Prime Minister Manuel Valls argued that his goal was to find a proper balance between the need to fight the terrorist threat in the context of the rule of law, he openly called upon the National Assembly to refrain from filing an appeal for cassation with the Constitutional Council (the country's highest constitutional authority) by pointing out the risk that the measures might be deemed unconstitutional and that the fight against terror superseded every other consideration.[8] Of the National Assembly, 551 of 558 ultimately voted in favour of the law. At the end of the day, Manuel Valls' request proved useless as the Constitutional Council determined in various decisions it made in 2016 and 2017 that despite the lack of balance between public safety and private freedom, the nullification of the measures would nonetheless have manifestly excessive consequences on public safety.[9] As a consequence, it meant that those who successfully managed to challenge some of the measures implemented in 2015 were unable to have them cancelled. The outcome was quite Kafkaesque: The National Assembly blindly approved the measures the executive branch requested that it validate and refused to challenge their lawfulness before the Constitutional Council, an institution that later chose to limit its own control over the question of people's natural rights by refusing to repeal legislation contrary to the principles it is supposed to uphold.

Secondly, the way these measures were implemented also contributed to their judicial control being rather theoretical and pointless. Indeed, very few individuals whose apartment or laptop the police searched or who were denied the right to participate in a protest chose to challenge the measures' lawfulness. Their decision was logically explained by the fact that there was no point in requesting the invalidation of a search that had already taken place or seeking to remove the ban on participating in an event that had been held months before. Furthermore, it was also revealed that these measures were used for means other than fighting terrorism as evidenced by the fact that individuals were banned from participating in public protests during the international conference on climate held in Paris in 2015 (Klausser, 2022, p. 216). Lastly, some individuals not connected with terrorism fell victim to these measures because of the preventive logic under which the measures were exercised. For instance, a man whose name appeared in a car theft investigation connected with the financing of Jihad who had also been seen taking pictures close to the residence of a *Charlie Hebdo* journalist was able to void his house arrest after proving that his mother lived in the same neighbourhood as the journalist, that the posture interpreted as him taking pictures was actually confused with him using the speakers on his phone while wearing a motorcycle helmet, and that his connection with the jihadist organisation was because he had been one of its victims (Klausser, 2022, p. 218). As it turned out, a thorough examination of the way the police were using these measures revealed that they relied more on suspicions than on facts, which led to innocent people facing serious and unjustified limitations on their individual freedom.

In other cases, especially in the United States, the legislative branch also adopted mechanisms that allowed a great margin of freedom to the president and the executive branch, such as the 1976 National Emergencies Act. US Congress also decided to grant George W. Bush tremendous exceptional powers through the Patriot Act and the Authorization for Use of Military Force, both of which were adopted with very little scrutiny in the days/weeks that followed the 9/11 attacks. Just like in the French case, a balance between civil liberties and public safety was not found, and civil liberties have been sacrificed on the altar of national security. Indeed, many measures that were initially part of the Patriot Act were later deemed unconstitutional by US courts, while the Authorization for Use of Military Force has effectively given the government a blank cheque allowing it to resort to the use of force against an unknown list of entities around the world.

What is striking about the legislative model of a state of exception is its capacity to produce liberticidal outcomes in what appears to be a more legitimate manner because its measures are *in fine* not the decision of one individual who is absolutely in charge but rather the result of a complex process that directly involves the representatives of the people: *Vox populi vox Dei*. However, this is just an impression since support of the legislative branch does not guarantee the people that their rights will enjoy better protection than would have been possible through the Roman-type model of dictatorship. Despite the fact that this legislative model is not a novelty in itself and was implemented and used way before what I have identified as the tectonic shift to a *homo superstes* understanding of human life (in 1991 with the fall of communism), this new biological conception of existence has increased encroachments on people's freedom through the implementation of disproportionate measures that are less and less temporary, a phenomenon that entails the risk of banalising extreme measures as acceptable. This is the outcome of a process that silences necessary questioning and dissent when it comes to limiting people's freedom. Indeed, because civil unrest is easily circumscribable in time and place, it is possible to ascertain with near certainty when such events are no longer posing imminent danger to public order and, accordingly, to end the state of emergency. This was the case in the fall of 2005 after the French government, with the approval of the National Assembly, resorted to extreme measures following the unrest in the suburbs of the country's big cities. Only a month after the measures were implemented on November 8, the State Council determined, on December 9, that the conditions that justified the state of emergency had evolved in a favourable direction and that these measures would no longer be required if the situation remained the same until the end of the year. Hence, the state of emergency was lifted on January 4 (Thénault, 2007, p. 76).

This is far from the case with more fluid menaces to our wellbeing and lives that are perpetual, unsolvable, and constantly hiding in the dark and waiting to strike against us when we least suspect it. This is clearly true of terrorism, which simply does not fit into the category of imminence as it is generally understood; this characteristic sparked confusion between 'pre-emptive' attacks and 'preventive' ones over the last 20 years. As I have already argued elsewhere (Caron, 2021a, 2023), unless some concrete information about an upcoming terrorist attack becomes available, what is lacking when it comes to terrorist groups is the impossibility to foresee where and when they will strike. Because of their modus operandi, these elusive enemies can covertly attack and kill thousands of civilians without any precursory signs. In fact, contrary to state actors planning to violate another state's sovereignty, terrorist groups do not display mass mobilisation of troops and military equipment near their enemy's borders. On the contrary, because of the asymmetrical nature of terrorists' fight against the great powers, their success relies on the element of surprise, which Noam Lubell summarised as follows:

> The challenge posed in the context of imminence is that, in effect, we are faced with a threat, for which we cannot positively identify how soon it might happen, where it will originate from, where it will strike, or even who precisely will be behind the attack. […] the threat of terrorism plays on the fear of the unknown, and raises the question of engaging in self-defense to prevent a possible future attack without knowledge of what it might be. As such, it challenges not so much the interpretation of imminence, but the effect calls into question the very existence of the imminence requirement. […] the idea of acting to prevent a vague and non-specific threat cannot, therefore, be covered within the concept of imminence.
>
> (2015, p. 707)

For this reason, the terrorist threat is feared as a constant one, a feeling reinforced when individuals use this type of political violence on a more or less regular basis, which only serves as a reminder that it is never gone, as has been in the case in France, starting in January 2015 with the attack against the *Charlie Hebdo* cartoonists and the Hypercacher grocery store siege and continuing with the disrupted attack in August on the Thalys train between Amsterdam and Paris, the November attacks at the Bataclan, the Stade de France, and other bars and terraces, the July 2016 ramming of pedestrians on the *Promenade des Anglais* in Nice with a 19-tonne cargo truck, and the December 2018 attack on people at the Strasbourg Christmas market by a single male assailant. When we add to this the fact that individuals feel that the state's most important obligation is to ensure their survival, we end up with a perfect storm where exceptional measures are becoming increasingly acceptable and normal in the minds of the people, who have gradually grown accustomed to them and thus accept extreme measures' permanent inclusion in their society's legal framework, especially when they only appear to have positive consequences. When people have the impression that exceptional measures have helped to deter terrorist attacks or when such measures make them feel safe, they quickly forget that the police may also read their personal communication and, believing that they are immune because they have not done anything wrong, people also fail to fathom themselves being mistakenly arrested or put under house arrest by a zealous police officer for unjustified reasons. Under these circumstances, people cultivate the belief that extreme measures cannot harm their personal freedom and are therefore completely acceptable – that is, until they are personally affected.

Furthermore, we also need to realise how difficult contesting exceptional measures can be for members of the legislative branch whose mandate depends on their belief that they ought to serve the people's best interest, a vision that can quickly become blurred by the results of polls and surveys. This creates a vicious circle involving the decay of liberal democracy as an outcome of the way in which it is functioning. Those in charge of adopting laws are expected to impose restrictions that will be proportionate to the objective they are trying to achieve and to shape laws that will cause the most limited harm to people's negative freedom. However, since legislators owe their mandates to the people who will live by these laws, it is easy for the former to impose measures that are beyond what is needed and required when the people are asking for them. It is needless to add that resisting these demands would likely result in the representatives being ousted from office at the first opportunity the people have to do so. In a situation dominated by the fear of dying (the actual chances of which tend to be highly exaggerated, as I have already mentioned) and especially in the aftermath of a terrorist attack when there is usually a 'rally around the flag' effect, members of the legislative branch have very little incentive to openly critically assess emergency legislation they are asked to approve (which they usually do in a matter of a few hours or days, without a thorough examination of the ins and outs). In other words, the irrational panic associated with these life-threatening menaces easily leads to hastily adopted disproportional measures that have been poorly evaluated and that people tend to gradually banalise as no longer exceptional but, on the contrary, rather reasonable and acceptable in a free and democratic society, especially when they are perceiving such measures as simple annoyances at the most.

78 *State of Emergency or a New Governance Paradigm*

If we leave aside the vicious circle of electoral democracy that plays a role in hindering individuals' freedom through the implementation of emergency measures, as well as the difficulty of determining when the threat that prompted the imposition of these measures is no longer imminent, I believe that there is something else utterly different between the *homo superstes* conception of life and the Lockean vision of liberalism that prevents the legislative branch from being more critical about the necessity of emergency measures. Since the *homo superstes* conception of life can only be assessed through a binary outlook (one is either alive or dead), the personal cost politicians could pay for opposing emergency measures is exponentially higher than when a Lockean vision of life prevails. Indeed, forgiveness is significantly more difficult to attain when refusal to act has led to people's death than when a similar course of action was taken with respect to a non-life-threatening menace. In these latter cases, individuals can always justify themselves by their willingness to act upon fundamental principles that are ultimately in the best interests of the people they represent. Such behaviour does not hinder their reputation or career in the long run, as was the case, for instance, with François Mitterrand who opposed the granting of full powers to de Gaulle in 1958.[10] This may explain why the legislative branch's adoption of emergency measures was, in the past, less consensual than it is now. The context has changed as the mirror of liberalism is no longer the fear of authoritarianism but rather the fear of death. For instance, when a state of emergency was first introduced in France in 1955, it was opposed by 255 members of the National Assembly, and in 1985, 141 opposed it in the context of the civil unrest in Polynesia, and in 2005, there were 148 in opposition. Nowadays, in our *homo superstes* world, measures for facing life-threatening emergencies are met with near unanimity among members of the legislative branch who, in the image of their co-citizens, are no longer motivated by higher philosophical principles aimed at limiting encroachments on individual freedom because they no longer perceive the uniqueness of their society in opposition to the abuse of authority (or they simply cannot afford the luxury of being principled in a Lockean manner as it would no longer resonate in the people's minds as being the most important feature of their liberal society).[11] If opponents are hailed as principled individuals and protectors of inalienable natural rights when a Lockean perspective dominates, they are now perceived as irresponsible and as denying others the right to enjoy what they consider to be their most important right, namely the right to live. When this is at stake in an environment where people are obnubilated by the fear of death, it is better to be judged for having shown an excess caution rather than to risk being ruined for having been overconfident in the face of potential danger.

The state of emergency imposed in liberal states during the COVID-19 pandemic exemplifies the aforementioned flaws in the legislative model of emergency measures when the *homo superstes* conception of existence dominates. Not only were these measures disproportional in light of the threat the societies were actually facing, but the measures also tended to lose their temporary nature and effectively led to the concentration of massive power in the hands of the executive branch with very little control – or none at all – being exercised on the part of members of the legislative branch. Similar to the terrorist threat, out of fear of dying from COVID-19,[12] individuals wanted their government to act swiftly in order to protect them, even if it came at the cost of severe restrictions on their freedoms, as they perceived these very same liberties – especially the freedoms of assembly and movement – as important vectors of contamination with what was falsely believed to be a highly deadly infection affecting all strata of the population.[13] What was astonishing about this situation was that people wanted these restrictions imposed not only on themselves but also on others.[14] As a result, for many months, millions of people living in liberal societies were denied basic liberties (and not mere privileges), such as the right to protest, to assemble, to leave their house (which was only allowed for a limited number of activities and within a very delimited area), to engage in outdoor activities, to worship according to their religious beliefs, and in the case of children and students, to enjoy basic and age-appropriate education.

Many also believe that the restrictive countermeasures ought to remain in place as individuals are still facing an imminent threat from COVID-19, which is not only not going to disappear from our lives but will constantly mutate into new variants that will keep evading the protection provided by the vaccines developed based on the original strain of the virus. As of the time of writing, less than three years since the start of the pandemic, societies are now (apparently) facing a tenth wave of contamination thanks to the XBB.1.5 variant (also known as the Kraken variant). Unsurprisingly, and as has been the case with many aspects of terrorism legislation,[15] many anti-COVID-19 measures that were initially promised to be temporary have become permanent.[16] This shift was predictable in light of the confrontation between a virus that is here to stay and people who have developed a *homo superstes* conception of life. Obviously, this can only lead to willingness to pass new laws that will banalise the exceptional by legalising through executive decrees, lockdowns, curfews, mandatory vaccination, mandatory masking, and the unnoticed and discretionary furloughing of employees – exceptional measures that previously required Parliament's approval. Very rarely does a state of emergency lead to a *status quo ante*. On the contrary, it tends to maintain exceptional measures by making them permanent. In a context where this type of governance is slowly but surely becoming less and less exceptional, this phenomenon is worrying to say the least (even more so when the fear of death dominates peoples' minds).

This pandemic has also allowed us to witness what I have previously described regarding the way people opposed to emergency measures have been treated, namely not as individuals with whom a majority of their co-citizens disagreed but nonetheless respected, as was the case when other states of emergencies were implemented in the twentieth century, but rather as irresponsible persons who posed a threat to others' lives and whose voices lacked all legitimacy and needed to be silenced. The general public has considered such persons' reasons for opposition to be the outcome of their belief in conspiracy theories or of a lack of education. It has been seen that statesmen did nothing to calm these insulting judgements that contributed to shutting down rational and nuanced debate about the emergency measures (debates that are impossible anyway when the binary outlook on a specific matter is either life or death in a world dominated by the *homo superstes* understanding of life). For instance, Dutch Prime Minister Mark Rutte called those opposing the reintroduction of lockdown 'idiots' in November 2021,[17] and in September 2021, Canadian Prime Minister Justin Trudeau called dissenters 'racist' and 'misogynistic extremists'[18] and openly asked if a democratic society could tolerate them. Similarly, French President Emmanuel Macron called dissenters victims of 'delirium'.[19] Inevitably, such comments led to deep social fracture between dissenters and compliers, with compliers seeing those who criticised the measures not only as a threat to their lives but also as responsible for their inability to return to their pre-COVID-19 way of life. This is, however, unsurprising when a *homo superstes* vision of human existence predominates, as its binary vision (life or death) excludes any form of compromise or middle ground and requires that non-compliers be viewed as dangerous extremists who must be treated harshly.

The Canadian government's use of the Emergencies Act in February 2022 is a good example in this regard. The law was activated following a demonstration where a convoy of truckers comprising an estimated 550–1,200 vehicles and between 3,000 and 18,000 people blocked the downtown Ottawa streets around Parliament Hill and staged a non-violent protest. Initially, a protest against the COVID-19 vaccination requirement for crossing the US–Canadian border, what became known as the 'freedom convoy' quickly evolved into a broad movement opposing the excesses of the COVID-19 countermeasures, with 'liberty' as its motto. The government's response was uncompromising as it chose to impose numerous measures of exception against the protest's organisers, participants, and those who financially supported the movement. Bank accounts were frozen and people were arrested, with some denied bail[20] despite the fact that the protest was non-violent and no weapons were found at the site.[21] Prime Minister Justin Trudeau claimed that invoking the Emergencies Act was necessary as the country was facing a national crisis,[22] a rationale that was severely attacked a few months later when testimonies from police and senior government officials in front of a public inquiry commission – that had to be established in accordance with the law – showed that that was simply not the case.[23] Despite these damning revelations, Canadians have remained largely supportive of their prime minister's decision. In a poll conducted in November 2022 after the commission had completed its hearings, 66% of Canadians said they were either supportive or somewhat supportive of Trudeau's actions.[24]

This attitude is symptomatic of a political environment where the Hobbesian viewpoint that consists of ensuring the protection of people's lives takes precedence over any other consideration. Whereas Lockean logic from the people would focus on evaluating the evidence supporting exceptional actions against any so-called threat in order to make sure that they are justified and proportionate, the former perspective relies upon an exaggeration of the threat that the people largely accept because they have integrated into their psyche the primal fear that life is all that matters. Anything that may delay what is thought necessary to survive or would result in inaction against a potential threat is automatically ruled as unacceptable, and no actions taken in the name of preserving life are deemed problematic.

We must also add that when a *homo superstes* understanding of life dominates in emergency situations thought to be life or death, nuances and open discussions about what to do are not possible before measures are implemented and after they have been enforced (especially in a context where the threat seems constant), which leads to a public sphere irreconcilably divided between two options that belong to two completely different worlds. The public is, as a consequence, unable to engage in a calm and respectful debate. When the desire to live dominates, it is uncompromising and unlimited in its aims and means and cannot fathom being restricted in light of any other considerations or principles. This is why the social fracture between proponents and opponents of the emergency measures that resulted from the COVID-19 pandemic was so severe and unique in comparison with the previous oppositions I have discussed. When the meaning of life was understood, during the Cold War, in a way where people's fears differed from those societies were facing, the semantics were the same on both sides. Individuals may have differed in terms of their respective understanding of freedom and the legitimate extent of their state's actions, but they talked about the same thing. Opponents to one's cause were simply thought to have a faulty way of appreciating the problem at hand, but at no point was their reasoning thought to be deficient to the point where entering into a dialogue with them was deemed worthless. In this context, even if de Gaulle and Mitterrand were politically opposed to one another, their opposition was philosophical in essence, and these two characters with huge personal egos were, nonetheless, able to respect each other as human beings. They did not perceive each other as an existential enemy but rather as an opponent whose point of view – though different – was, nonetheless, considered a

State of Emergency or a New Governance Paradigm 83

constitutive and necessary part of the democratic agonistic process. When this is the case, disagreements will exist, but they will not degenerate into a lack of respect that will take the form of censorship, threats, and any other measures meant to silence the other party whose voice is excluded from the public sphere as unpatriotic or perverted by conspiracy theories. It is, however, completely different when one side is perceiving the other side as a life-threatening danger. In such cases, as Chantal Mouffe (1994) argued, our contradictor is no longer seen as an opponent but rather as an enemy that needs to be stopped and against whom almost all countermeasures are deemed appropriate. This is because the opposition is the result of two completely separate logics based on two different sets of values, which makes these two systems irreconcilable and renders normal democratic agonism impossible. In place of it, political violence – a soft version of it, obviously – takes over. This opposition aims at shutting out pluralism by diabolising those from the other side as mutually disrespectful proponents of these two value systems. Regardless of the ideas supporting the claims of the one the other perceives as a life-threatening danger, the one who feels threatened is unable to find any value in those ideas as the Hobbesian desire to remain alive is unyielding and makes believers willing to tolerate restrictions those who abide by a Lockean view of liberalism are less inclined to accept. In such situations, victory over one's opponent in the form of the adoption of stringent emergency measures is insufficient to eliminate the threat the dissident poses, since dissidents' very existence is perceived as the real threat, especially when they refuse to comply with the measures. This transforms the nature of the menace and the way people believe it ought to be fought, namely in an uncompromising fashion that aims at making dissidents' lives miserable.[25] This has been the case during the COVID-19 pandemic, with non-compliers being threatened with the withholding of medical treatment or termination of their work contract. Sadly enough, there was also a similar reaction to people who were critical of America's war against terror following 9/11. University faculty teaching about and researching international relations were expected to show explicit support for America's foreign policy in return for public funding,[26] and journalists called domestic opposition to the war against terror 'immoral'.[27] In societies where the *homo superstes* conception of human life predominates, tolerance of ideas or positions considered to be life-threatening (or fuelling such menaces) is non-existent and a spirit of vengeance, punishment, and censorship takes over in a way that is far from being reasonable in a liberal society.

Conclusion

As argued in this chapter, the shift towards a *homo superstes* understanding of human life is by no means an inconsequential matter, as it has opened the door to a new form of governance that has banalised resorting to exceptional measures. This has been neglected by many for several years since this type of governance dominated by emergencies has taken root in a political practice that not only existed prior to this evolution of our meaning of life but that also relies (at least, in theory) on the key participation of the legislative power. However, this evolution from a constitutional practice as old as politics itself has, nonetheless, engendered tremendous consequences for the civil concord of Western societies and people's former relationship with their state, resulting in the people becoming less distrustful of their statesmen, a mistake that can only lead to liberticidal practices.

Unlike the principle-based opposition that was once at the heart of the imposition of a state of emergency, the fear of dying has created a situation that sends debates in an uncompromising direction that is unable to tolerate any nuances or dissidence. This makes the emergencies of today more destructive from a societal perspective than those in the past where people used the same vocabulary despite disagreeing with one another. This can no longer be the case with our contemporary emergencies that are thought to be life-threatening, as the semantics that crystallise opposition in the public sphere now belong to two different worlds that are incompatible with one another. This has led to the emergence of an uncompromising reality based on two radically different conceptions of what society ought to be, which has revealed the illiberal face of liberalism, that is, the possibility that a liberal society may, under these circumstances, consider soft violence and intolerance to be legitimate in order to silence a point of view deemed dangerous for the well-being of the people and of the society at large. This becomes acceptable when the one with whom we disagree is no longer considered to be an opponent, a logic that contains the seeds of the decay of liberalism through triggering of the use of oppressive force against those cast as unwanted enemies.

Furthermore, because the emergencies of the past were easily circumscribable in space and time, they were temporary, and the same has historically been thought about emergency measures. This is no longer the case with the types of menaces that have arisen under the *homo superstes* perspective. Evasive, always hiding in the dark waiting to strike at us when we least suspect it, and unstoppable despite our best efforts, these threats are permanent, which can only serve to transform the temporary emergency measures of yesterday into permanent ones. This situation is not to be taken lightly as it bears a lot of similarity to what Carl Schmitt once described as 'sovereign dictatorships' that allow a few individuals to hijack democracy. However, amazingly, very few people seem to see the problem here, as the transformative measures implemented to save our lives from terrorists or a respiratory virus were demanded and welcomed by a significant and very vocal majority. The resultant erosion of individual freedom has been eclipsed by another need that is considered superior, namely remaining alive.

This highlights how liberal societies have entered into a new evolutionary phase that will lead them to become increasingly less liberal with time. As I have said, one of the main conditions for the survival of individual freedom has always been necessary distrust between citizens and those chosen to make decisions in their name. This tension has forced representatives to refrain from going overboard with measures that could prove detrimental to the people's natural rights. Fear of corruption arising from representatives prioritising their private interests over the general interest was a healthy apprehension that ultimately ensured the preservation of people's freedom. The defiance of yesterday has, however, given way to a form of blind trust in state authorities once the fear of dying takes over. Perceived as the only ones able to guarantee the safety of the people, individuals entrust institutions and their representatives to do whatever is deemed necessary. In other words, unlike before, when the state was considered a potential threat, it is now perceived, in a *homo superstes* world, as the saviour. This shift risks creating 'nannyism' logic, where individuals tend to consider themselves less as citizens and more as minors or subjects. This novel form of 'soft despotism' is, unfortunately, reassuring and not troubling to people whose view of life has shrunk to its mere biological dimension. Ultimately, however, the price to pay is the decay of the true meaning of liberalism in favour of a Hobbesian-like version that is falsely believed to be liberal but actually has more to do with authoritarianism than democracy.

Notes

1 It is difficult to provide a comprehensive and explicit list of what can constitute an emergency as every situation must be assessed with respect to its specificities. We are therefore left with definitions such as this one from John Ferejohn and Pasquale Pasquino:

> What makes a circumstance exceptional? Sometimes there is a special need for speed or decisional efficiency. Armies need to be created and supplied and moved rapidly from place to place. Some areas of the country might need to be abandoned, and there may be little time to listen to objections from the residents. Or, there may be special needs for secrecy so that opponents will be unable to learn of the nation's aims or plans. Or, there may be a need to stabilize the constitutional system against the nefarious efforts of its enemies. Each of these needs might be met by suspending rights of speech, assembly, and notice that are normally protected constitutionally.
>
> (2004, pp. 220–221)

2 He wrote the following in his *Two Treatises*:

> Constant frequent meetings of the legislative, and long continuations of their assemblies, without necessary occasion, could not but be burdensome to the people, and must necessarily in time produce more dangerous inconveniencies, and yet the quick turn of affairs might be sometimes such as to need their present help; any delay of their convening might endanger the public; and sometimes too their business might be so great, that the limited time of their sitting might be too short for their work, and rob the public of that benefit which could be had only from their mature deliberation. What then could be done in this case to prevent the community from being exposed some time or other to eminent hazard, on one side or the other, by fixed intervals and periods, set to the meeting and acting of the legislative; but to entrust it to the prudence of some, who being present, and acquainted with the state of public affairs, might make use of this prerogative for the public good? And where else could this be so well placed as in his hands, who was entrusted with the execution of

the laws for the same end? Thus supposing the regulation of times for the assembling and sitting of the legislative not settled by the original constitution, it naturally fell into the hands of the executive, not as an arbitrary power depending on his good pleasure, but with this trust always to have it exercised only for the public weal, as the occurrences of times and change of affairs might require.

(chap. XIII, sec. 156)

3 Marc de Wilde wrote:

The story of Cincinnatus's commitment to the republic and his willingness to give up his powers as soon as he had fulfilled his task was intended to illustrate the ethical qualities that were expected of a dictator: [H]e was expected to be virtuous and trustworthy, committed to the safety of Rome and the preservation of its republican institutions. [...] the virtues Cincinnatus displayed as a dictator – the fidelity to republican institutions, the willingness to make his own private interests subservient to the public good, the commitment to protect those dependent on his power – were all part of his *fides* or trust. In the late roman Republic, the *fides* was considered a fundamental norm and general standard of behaviour for magistrates, incorporating the expectation that they exercised their power in good faith, not to pursue their own interests, but to promote the public good.

(2012, pp. 563–564)

4 In that sense, the granting of full powers to de Gaulle in 1958 is probably the last contemporary example of a genuine Roman type of dictatorship. In contrast, his use of emergency powers in 1961 was not the result of him having been granted this possibility because of his virtues or talents but rather because he held the position of head of state that allowed him to do so through constitutional means.
5 Following the criminal burning of the Reichstag on February 27, 1933, Hitler requested that President Hindenburg declare a state of emergency on the following day in accordance with Article 48 of Germany's Basic Law of 1919 that allowed the government to curtail constitutional rights. Since this decree was never repealed, Nazi rule was, from that date until its total collapse in May 1945, a state of exception.
6 Although it states that, before triggering the political tools of Article 16, the president needs to consult the prime minister, the president of the National Assembly, the president of the Senate, and the Constitutional Council, the president is not required to obtain their support.

7 This latter point is eminently problematic and is not comparable with Roman dictatorship, which was rather 'commissarial', to use Carl Schmitt's (2014) expression. This type of exceptionalism was not aimed at transforming the constitutional order but was rather inherently conservative by nature and designed with the sole purpose of saving it, whereas the legislative model is 'sovereign' and designed to create a different constitutional and legal order.
8 www.politis.fr/articles/2015/11/etat-durgence-valls-admet-ne-pas-respecter-la-constitution-33107/
9 Decision no. 2016-567/568 QPC, September 23, 2016; no. 2016-600 QPC, December 2, 2016; M. Raïme A.; no. 2017-635 QPC, June 9, 2017; no. 2017-677 QPC, December 1, 2017.
10 He even wrote a book about it (1964).
11 In 2015, the state of emergency was opposed by only seven members of the French National Assembly and only 67 members of the US Congress (66 from the House of Representatives and one from the Senate) out of its 535 members (435 representatives and 100 senators).
12 For instance, in Italy, the fear of contracting COVID-19 dropped below 50% in June 2021 but had risen above that figure once more by February 2022. In Canada, the figure was below 50% in May 2020, July 2020, and September 2020. Outside these short periods of time, it remained above that percentage from March 2020 until February 2021. That fear reached 88% in Japan in April 2020 and remained very high (between 72% and 80%) until March 2021. https://yougov.co.uk/topics/international/articles-reports/2020/03/17/fear-catching-Covid-19
13 Support for COVID-19 countermeasures such as mandatory quarantine for anyone who was in contact with a contaminated patient, cancellation of large events, and quarantining of individuals arriving from abroad remained above 50% for months throughout the pandemic in countries like Canada, Australia, Germany, Great Britain, and Italy. https://yougov.co.uk/topics/international/articles-reports/2020/03/17/level-support-actions-governments-could-take
14 British barrister Francis Hoar said, 'What is terrifying is that this wasn't just imposed by governments[;] people wanted it. Of course people can choose to stay in their homes, but they wanted it to be law, to impose these restrictions on others' (qtd. in Dodsworth, 2021, p. 226).
15 This is what happened when France lifted the state of emergency in October, 719 days after the Paris terrorist attacks. However, the following day, the Code of Homeland Security (*Code de la sécurité intérieure*) was modified to normalise the exceptional measures introduced in 2015.
16 www.bbc.com/news/uk-scotland-scotland-politics-61969639

17 The expression 'Covidiots' became widespread during the pandemic in the general population.
18 www.westernstandard.news/news/trudeau-calls-the-unvaccinated-racist-and-misogynistic-extremists/article_a3bacece-2e14-5b8c-bf37-eddd672205f3.html
19 www.liberation.fr/checknews/misogynes-et-racistes-justin-trudeau-a-t-il-lui-aussi-insulte-les-non-vaccines-20220105_QSJGYSMLRFG3NMDXNMGWCJNPHE/
20 One individual, Tyson Billings, a vocal opponent of COVID-19 countermeasures, spent 116 days in jail before being released after pleading guilty to a count of inciting people to commit mischief. Tamara Lich, one of the organisers of the freedom convoy, faced months of criminal procedures in the aftermath of the protest.
21 https://tnc.news/2022/03/24/ottawa-police-chief-admits-no-firearms-discovered-at-freedom-convoy/
22 By definition, according to Canadian law, this refers to espionage, plans to overthrow the government, and threats or acts of serious violence to achieve political, religious, or ideological ends.
23 www.politico.com/news/2022/11/20/trudeau-emergencies-act-freedom-convoy-00069651
24 www.theglobeandmail.com/politics/article-emergencies-act-poll-favour/
25 We can recall French President Emmanuel Macron's promise to 'piss off (*emmerder*) those who refused to comply with the rules' and New Zealand Prime Minister Chris Hipkins' threat in an interview to 'chase out and look for the non-compliers'.
26 'Americans for Victory Over Terrorism', *New York Times*, March 16, 2002; Michelle Goldberg, 'Osama University?', *Salon*, November 6, 2003; Michael Dobbs, 'Middle East Studies Under Scrutiny in US', *Washington Post*, January 13, 2004.
27 Peter Beinart, 'Sidelines', *The New Republic*, September 24, 2001.

4 Recapturing Freedom

The picture I have painted so far is indeed a dark one, and the question that now needs to be answered is what we can do to recapture freedom, which is inextricably running away from us, with our consent. Although this is obviously not an easy task, it is, nonetheless, not an unfeasible one. What I would like to do in this last chapter is to present a few solutions in this regard as a sketch of how to recapture the genuine meaning of human life from a liberal perspective, that is, in a way that would foster our negative freedom by making us less dependent on the state and by offering the opportunity to rejuvenate active citizenship in a way that would not result in the total submission of the individual's interests to those of the collective.

As I described briefly in the first part of this book, the presence of constitutional guarantees that protect people's individual freedoms in liberal societies is a rather limited way of assessing the extent to which we can enjoy our negative freedom. In this case, theory offers a very imprecise view of this question since, from an empirical perspective, individual freedom can end up being as limited as in authoritarian regimes thanks to social tyranny, or measures can result in detrimental impacts on people's professional future. When individuals are facing these two sorts of undue pressure, their margin of freedom can shrink dramatically to the point where conformism ends up being their only possible alternative. When this is happening, the fear of being ostracised or of losing one's job takes over, and individuals constrain their freedom to say certain things or to pursue certain courses of

DOI: 10.4324/9781003387749-5

action. Such self-restraint has been visible during the COVID-19 pandemic, where vaccination – though not mandatory – nonetheless felt compulsory since it conditioned, in a very significant manner, people's capacity to enjoy freedom and, more importantly, to work. Therefore, the question is whether it is possible to reduce these vulnerabilities that can erase the boundaries between tyranny and democracy when it comes to the actual enjoyment of freedom.

It is generally assumed, in a very Lockean fashion, that freedom is best guaranteed when the state's capacity to interfere in our lives is as fragmented as possible, namely through the presence of various counter-powers, the devolution of powers in various substate entities (federalism or other forms of decentralisation being seen as optimal solutions in this regard), or thanks to the Bill of Rights that strictly forbids the state from infringing on our negative freedom. This was the mindset of the drafters of the American constitution, who believed, in the manner of James Madison, that tyranny is only possible in the absence of such safeguards and when all political powers are concentrated in the same hands (Hamilton et al., 2009, p. 101). This opinion is what defines the view many hold that liberal democracy is inherently more able to allow people to enjoy their freedom than authoritarian regimes where this division of power does not exist. So, yes, in theory, such mechanisms make it impossible for one state official to censor people, throw them in jail without due process and without reason, or impose an orthodox viewpoint on citizens and punish them when they do not abide by it. This explains why liberal states are wary of states of emergency and have largely favoured the legislative model rather than its Roman counterpart in exceptional cases when needed. This view is, unfortunately, inaccurate, as I have shown throughout this book, since it neglects the three other factors that can end up limiting people's freedom despite these constitutional guarantees, namely social tyranny, our connection with work and the role it plays in our lives, as well as the *homo superstes* understanding of human existence.

Indeed, in theory, limitations on the state's capacity to interfere in our choices have allowed for the emergence of a pluralistic civil society defined by people's ability to express their opinions and freely join other like-minded individuals. Because civil society stands as an independent sphere distinct from the government, it is believed to ensure full individual freedom, as the sole menace to negative freedom is thought to lie in the concentration of political power. However, as I have already explained, this sphere has, nonetheless, developed the capacity to radically repress people's actions by threatening them with social ostracism, with being deprived of a job promotion, or with not being able to find a job at all when they publicly express marginal and critical opinions. In a way, out of fear of the state, liberalism has created a space that was meant to allow individuals to enjoy their freedom but has not provided the proper mechanisms that would prevent organisations or groups of people from infringing in numerous ways on the freedom of those who happen to disagree with the majority. As a result, what was fundamentally a good intention has transformed into a nightmare for countless individuals whom civil society has punished or who have, to avoid being punished, chosen to conform and silence their beliefs out of fear of facing the terrible consequences of this social tyranny that no authority can stop (since the civil sphere is independent and beyond the state's control).

When de Tocqueville first discussed this notion, the fear of social tyranny was attributed to people's psychological reluctance to risk ostracisation in order to uphold a marginal and unpopular viewpoint. People's desperate need to be part of a group leads them to wilfully relinquish their freedom by choosing to conform to the dominant doxa because dissidence comes at too high a price. What the COVID-19 pandemic has shown us, however, is that there was clear willingness on the part of a very vocal minority that openly challenged the general rules enacted by their state even if the costs were facing strong criticism, mockery, and threats from the obedient majority and having to sever ties with their family[1] and friends (McBain, 2020). Therefore, it seems as though Tocquevillian repression of one's beliefs to avoid facing popular punishment and reprobation may not be an appealing option for many who would instead choose to act otherwise. How can we explain that? This could be attributable to the fact that we are now witnessing a clash between a Lockean minority and what appears to be the majority holding a *homo superstes* understanding of human life. As such, because the minority group sees it as a matter of principle, they, as the embodiment of the dominant Cold War-era interpretation of life, are now facing a type of governance and style of policy that are incompatible with what today's majority perceive as what ought to be the state's new role. As I said earlier, this can only lead to an uncompromising clash between the two groups that is far from peaceful or respectful. For those I call the Lockeans, opposing this novel way of conceiving human existence is not as trivial as refraining from opposing, denouncing, or criticising something of lesser importance that might offend public opinion. This is not the case with regard to everything associated with the Hobbesian understanding of life that threatens, in the Lockeans' eyes, the essence of their viewpoint on politics and their relationship with their state. In other words, even 30 years after the end of the Cold War and the appearance of the *homo superstes* conception of life, the old logic is still alive and active. As the old logic is incompatible with the new one, it is normal for us to see so many people express their dissidence even given the social ostracism attached to it, as such people see giving way to social tyranny as abdication of that in which they sincerely believe and as surrender on matters on which they are unwilling to compromise. Faithful to the former logic that prevailed during the Cold War, these individuals have the capacity and willingness to sacrifice substantially when they believe that the enjoyment of their freedom is at stake, which makes them as fierce and uncompromising as their Hobbesian counterparts.

There is no reason to expect any change to that opposition between contemporary Lockeans and Hobbesians as long as the former's conception remains vivid in the minds of many people despite the dominance of the *homo superstes* view of human existence. From this perspective, when other life-threatening menaces arise in the future, we may expect a similar violent opposition between those expecting and asking for extreme measures out of a fear of dying and those opposed to them because they feel that the measures are disproportionally liberticidal. This uncompromising opposition may not be the result of a simple rise of populism as it is often said or of social media contributing to the circulation of fake news, which, according to liberticidal logic, ought to justify state regulation of online platforms, thereby opening the door to undesirable censorship.[2] Rather than being the source of the problem (which may lie elsewhere in the more profound and incompatible opposition between the Lockean and Hobbesian conceptions of liberalism that have derived divergent understandings of human existence), social media platforms are tools that can make it easier for opponents of the dominant doxa to mobilise, leading to the creation of communities of interest among them that can, in turn, contribute to alleviating dissidents' isolation from some of their friends and family. In these sorts of opposition, the fear of social tyranny is clearly insufficient to prevent many individuals from speaking out and actively opposing their state – as is expected of Lockeans – so that is not the issue here. What is problematic is how this extreme lack of tolerance for other people's beliefs – which is reciprocal, it must be said – extends into the political realm and leads to unresolvable tensions that can even fuel violence since Lockeans may end up concluding that the disproportionate and liberticidal measures they are being forced to abide by justify the exercise of their right to resist.[3]

There is, however, room for optimism and hope that the *homo superstes* conception of human existence will fade away in favour of a return to the Cold War Lockean view of both humankind and the people's relationship with the state. There are many reasons to believe that the February 2022 Russian invasion of Ukraine will result in a major shift in world politics, and it is fair to say that the world has now entered – according to Thomas Kuhn's theory – a period of crisis between two paradigms. If the *coup de grâce* has been delivered to the post-Cold War paradigm of a world converging around liberal ideals (Caron, 2022c; Ikenberry, 2020; Wright, 2017) including human security, we are still unsure about the nature of the new paradigm that is yet to emerge. The best guess, at the moment, however, is the unfolding of a new opposition between a liberal and an illiberal world held together around a Moscow–Beijing axis. If this were to happen, liberalism may, once again, be able to define its uniqueness and superiority in relation to its new global enemy whose main political attributes are akin to authoritarianism.

The second type of tyrannical element that makes us vulnerable and can lead us to limit our own negative freedom is related to our dependency on our professional occupation due to the framing of the 'work paradigm' in our minds. As stated, because we link one of the main sources of our personal happiness and identity with our work, it has become tremendously easy for any person or entity to control the individual. Work has therefore become, over time, more than just a means of acquiring enough resources to survive and enjoy the undeniable perks of materialism; rather, it has become the central activity that allows us to imbue our lives with purpose, which is why unemployment is often perceived as a life tragedy. To avoid facing this catastrophic misfortune, many do not hesitate to accept what they would refuse to do under different circumstances, which is why Alexander Hamilton was right to point out that 'Power over a man's subsistence is power over his will'. Whereas the obvious question seems to be whether overcoming this work paradigm is possible, what we may actually have to wonder is simply whether this paradigm has a future. Indeed, the fourth industrial revolution is seriously challenging our relationship with work since many of us are under threat of losing our job to a machine. How many of us will be affected by this technological evolution fuelled by artificial intelligence (AI)? It is hard to say, but various studies have shown that it could directly affect between 25% and 50% of workers, or up to 80% of workers if we include in the calculation the impacts of displacement and wage suppression (Arntz et al., 2016; Berriman & Hawksworth, 2017; Ford, 2015; Frey & Osborne, 2013; Lee, 2018). What is unique about this revolution compared with the previous one that affected low-skilled employment is that the one we are currently facing is also threatening skilled jobs such as surgeons and radiologists thanks to the amazing and rapid advancement of nanotechnology. The outcome is easy to foresee: If unemployment was previously a short-term phenomenon, as laid-off workers had the capacity to find a new job by undergoing additional training or earning a degree of specialisation that allowed them to reintegrate into the sector of the job market demanding such skills, this may no longer be the case in the future. As the number of jobs being made redundant due to machine automation will affect both extremes of the work spectrum, the result will be a job shortage exclusively in the domain of human activities. If the predictions of the technological unemployment thesis (Susskind, 2018) are correct, advanced industrial societies may face mass unemployment sooner than they think, which will obviously deepen inequality and impact the survival of capitalism, which relies on mass consumption – something that will be no longer possible when people are jobless, as machines do not buy what they produce. If we think about this scenario from the dominant perspective that tends to equate our job with who we are and position our occupation as the basis of our individual happiness, what is forthcoming is certainly tragic. Far from just being a crisis of how we will survive without a salary (which will disappear as more and more of us become unemployed), it is, in fact, also a crisis of meaning concerning who we are and what gives meaning to our lives. Such a crisis will come with significant problems that should not be taken lightly, as Kay-Fu Lee has reminded us:

> Rates of depression triple among those unemployed for six months, and people looking for work are twice as likely to commit suicide as the gainfully employed. Alcohol abuse and opioid overdoses both rise alongside unemployed rates, with some scholars attributing rising mortality rates among uneducated white Americans to declining economic outcomes, a phenomenon they call 'deaths of despair'. The psychological damage of AI-induced unemployment will cut even deeper. People will face the prospect of not just being temporarily out of work but of being permanently excluded from the functioning of the economy. They will watch as algorithms and robots easily outperform them at tasks and skills they spent their whole lives mastering. It will lead to a crushing feeling of futility, a sense of having become obsolete in one's own skin.
>
> (2016, pp. 173–174)

However, similar to the previous situation, there is room for prudent optimism as this phenomenon may allow us to dissociate ourselves from our work and gain another way of giving meaning to our existence that would make us less vulnerable to being manipulated into doing things we may otherwise prefer not to do. We may either fall into despair or see the potential of this outcome that will strike millions of us by default when we are gradually replaced by robots and left unable to find another job as demand will largely outpace availability. If we choose the latter path, long-term or permanent AI-induced unemployment might indeed offer us the time to pursue unconventional work-related tasks and, through this, favour activities that will allow us to imbue our lives with meaning (from a source other than one's occupation) and ultimately find happiness and freedom. These activities could be those we have been neglecting because we have been hyper focusing our time and attention on our work. These activities waiting to be discovered may prove to be meaningful to us, fun, and uplifting. These could take various forms such as spending more time with our loved ones, playing a sport, getting involved in other hobbies, or becoming more actively involved in the public sphere. What this means is that perhaps our fate of becoming *homo laborans* is not irremediable after all. Not only is it currently contributing to making us vulnerable to other people's will, it is also an alienating process that unduly restricts personal happiness and our capacity to give ourselves a unique identity. This potential may be difficult to fully consider since the work paradigm has tended to oppose work to idleness, thereby associating any non-work-related activities with an improper lifestyle subject to the stigmas currently associated with unemployment, including laziness, a lack of work ethics, and vegging out without any goals. Thinking otherwise might take time and would certainly be very difficult, but the current technological revolution may not give us any alternative. However, if we see the glass as being half full rather than half empty, the future that awaits humans may be brighter than we think, especially when it comes to the question of personal freedom and not being leashed and led to take certain unwanted courses of action out of fear of losing our job.[4] Humankind may have a lot to gain from this technological revolution that bears the promise of freedom through the transformation of advanced industrial societies into *pensionopolis* that, unlike their Greek predecessors, do not require slavery or the exclusion of women from politics.

Apart from these considerations that are largely reliant on hopes, what can liberal societies do now – if they wanted to, of course – to fight off or minimise the impact of their new way of assessing human existence, which has come full circle during the COVID-19 pandemic after nearly 30 years of development, has on us, especially our individual freedom? I will offer my humble opinion in this regard, which, I am fully aware, may not be satisfactory to many readers. As I argued in Chapter 1, political modernity has ushered in an era of biopolitics by sacralising, in theory, individual rights, which has ultimately led to a post-heroic life that has made individuals afraid of anything that could hinder their self-expression. As I have just explained, this made us dependent on our job and caused a decline in courage, with the fear of dying overtaking every other consideration. In both cases, these two situations have made us more easily controllable. However, despite the fact that this revolution occurred more than 300 years ago, these effects have only recently shown their full potential. During that period of time, the ill effects of biopolitics have been offset by various types of 'ghosts', whether religious or secular, with the most important idea in light of what I have been analysing in this book being the way liberalism understood itself during the Cold War. With the 'end of history' however, that last dam that was able to contain the destabilising flow of biopolitics has been destroyed and replaced by a view of life that is entirely compatible with what biopolitics stands for, with the result being that it has allowed the *homo superstes* conception of life to blossom without any restrictions. However, this is only one of many casualties of biopolitics with an instrumental impact on people's willingness to show responsible citizenship when circumstances require it. There is also a tendency to see the public sphere simply as an instrument that allows us to enhance our private interests, thereby subordinating the general interest to peculiar individual objectives and transforming politics into a world that no longer has common points of reference.

If the possible resurgence of a Cold War type of liberalism of fear that could, once again, offset the forces of biopolitics and return us to Lockean liberalism is only a hope at the moment, we ought to keep in mind that biopolitics can be put in check despite the fact that liberal societies have enshrined negative freedom as one of their most important pillars. It may be possible, then, to think of mechanisms that could counter-balance such societies' problems without, of course, falling into the other extreme that would result in hindering people's freedom by subordinating them entirely to the interests of their communities. The objective is – if it is ever possible to achieve – to find a way to protect people's individual freedom and their right to life without transforming the latter notion into the sole and non-negotiable end one should be looking to achieve. The aim is rather to relativise the importance of biological life to re-energise a form of active citizenship that would recreate the pre-1991 world where the dynamic between the state and its citizens was more horizontal and less hasty in terms of the state imposing undue restrictions on citizens' freedom.

This is easier said than done because the main problem is to determine what ought to lead individuals to active involvement to protect their freedom. This is possible when their common understanding of their society depends primarily on the value of liberty over tyranny. In this case, their main fear of being deprived of what is of the highest importance to them will offset the impacts of biopolitics and prevent them from adopting a *homo superstes* conception of life. In other words, it comes down to the tautologic argument that people will defend their personal freedom insofar as they value their personal freedom. This is not a satisfactory way of thinking about how the relativisation of biological life may be achieved. Hence, we are back to square one, trying to determine how people can accept this and develop a less passive and infantilising attitude towards their state, which should value the defence of individual freedom without being able to rely on the type of fear that was dominant prior to liberalism proving its superiority over tyrannical forms of government some 30 years ago. How else can this be achieved? This is the Gordian knot of the problem: to make people value their liberty rather than their biological life in the absence of a system that thinks of itself and its superiority as the quintessential example of individual freedom.

The sole option left to consider requires rethinking the relationship liberal societies have operated in the last 300 years between biological life and politics as a way to offset the impacts and influence of the post-1991 liberalism of fear, since we may very well presuppose that its *homo superstes* seed would not have been able to flourish in unfertile soil. Indeed, that people have been able to integrate so quickly into their psyche the idea that biological life must prevail over any other political considerations may not be divorced from the fact that they were already psychologically prepared to accept this shift after prolonged evolution in a biopolitical world. In this sense, by limiting the attractiveness of biopolitics, the hope is that it will end up having the same impact on the *homo superstes* conception of life by disconnecting that with which is it associated from people's view of the meaning and significance of politics. This may be achieved by figuring out ways that would decentre humans from themselves by giving them a political dimension, resulting in the separation of the biological body from the political one. Because biopolitics is the result of the primacy of individuals' rights taking over the public sphere, there is a need to separate, once again, the world of *oikos* from the political realm, so that the latter can stop being perceived as something more substantial than what it is today, that is, a largely apolitical domain, the sole objective of which is ensuring people's capacity to pursue everything associated with their conception of happiness – with the protection of life being the most important right that conditions all others. If this can be achieved, people might be able to develop a civic conscience that would contribute to detaching them from the reductive *zóé* and highly individualistic viewpoint of life they have, with the advantage that this renewed sense of civicism might lead them to develop behaviours and attitudes that no longer require state intervention. Allow me to explain what I mean by that.

Despite its capacity to prevent the state from interfering unjustly with our freedom through a dynamic of distrust between officials in charge and citizens, the Lockean citizenry–statesmen dynamic remains, nonetheless, inherently flawed. It is flawed because, as I have explained, its efficiency depends on people privileging their individual freedom over any other consideration. When this is no longer the case and people start giving more weight to their mere survival, that dynamic simply collapses and is quickly replaced by a Hobbesian logic that relies on people's passive obedience. The fragility of this model, which can easily transit into liberticidal policies, rests in the fact that individuals are left outside the sphere of politics and are only considered watchmen (in the Lockean paradigm) or subjects who are expected to comply with rules enacted for the sake of their survival (in the Hobbesian paradigm). Hence, what is holding the Lockean dynamic in place as a system able to protect people's rights is an external element. However, if people's conception of politics was less reactive or passive and more active, it would empower them and make them less reliant on their representatives to make decisions in their name. Instead, they would not only be the ones telling government officials what to do, they would also be more conscious of the 'others' around them thanks to a more developed sense of community, thus allowing them to themselves restrict some of their actions in times of crisis as well as in more peaceful times without having to be told or ordered to do so.

The assumption here is that people's obsession with their own individuality, rights, and fear of death is ultimately what makes them less sensitive to their co-citizens' rights and more prone to expect and ask for the implementation of measures that may be disproportionate to the actual threat. As long as such measures make certain people feel safe or guarantee that their rights will be respected, it will not matter if the same measures negatively hinder the rights of others. In this regard, neither the Lockean nor the Hobbesian model is immune from these excesses because of the individualistic premise on which they are established. However, caring about what impacts our requests may have on others brings a sense of well-needed moderation because people will have to suddenly stop considering themselves as sacred individuals entitled to enjoy all the rights nature has endowed and also consider their parallel political identity or body as fraternal members of a shared community. Furthermore, through this sense of community, individuals will be able to regulate their behaviours in a way that would be more respectful of their freedoms and those of others. Restraint would, in this sense, emanate from the people themselves and would be more proportionate than when it is coming from an external actor solely based upon what we perceive as our own particular best interest when we are tending toward perceiving ourselves as sacred individuals.

In a way, this dual system of bodies – ourselves as unique entities able to enjoy basic natural rights and awareness of our belonging to a broader community – looks to reproduce the family model on a broader scale. As parents, spouses, sons/daughters, and brothers/sisters, we are all aware that our inalienable freedom needs to take into consideration the impacts of our actions on our kin. Of course, we may disagree and argue, but these natural ties we share with our close ones lead us to compromise without needing an external actor to intervene and tell us what to do. These tradeoffs offer the best possible balance between the expectations of our two bodies. By extending these family connections to the broader community, citizens' self-regulation and willingness to take others' concerns into account might serve as a guarantee for respect for everybody's interests in a moderate and balanced manner. How can this be implemented? The answer is through a system of passive and active rights that separates political rights from the simple fact of our biological life, thereby refraining from making political sovereignty dependent upon people's birth. More precisely, the constitutional protection of passive rights (e.g. the right to life, to pursue one's conception of happiness, and all other basic natural rights) would not automatically allow individuals to enjoy their active rights, which are political by nature (and are connected with their ability to directly influence the democratic process). To acquire these rights, individuals would have to undergo a public-spirited process of collective acculturation that might take the form of military or national service and involvement in other long-term charity work. Inspired by Abbé Sieyès, the famous author of *What Is the Third Estate?*, a proposal submitted to the National Assembly in July 1789, the idea of not linking active citizenship with the simple fact of birth should not aim at excluding parts of the population, as Sieyès suggested, based on unacceptable reasons, such as the so-called educational vices of women, as suggested 4 years later in Jean-Denis Lanjuinais' *Conventionel* (Wallerstein, 2003, p. 654). Nobody ought to be excluded from enjoying their political rights as it would depend entirely on people's willingness to develop a second body in parallel to their biological one.

Would it be sufficient to generate a civic-minded citizenry strong enough to offset the overdominance of biopolitics in a situation where individuals living in liberal societies no longer think about their political system's exceptionalism in terms of preserving individual rights but rather as ensuring their survival? It is hard to say, just like any other theoretical proposal, but anything that could offset self-centred individualism that leads to the creation of wizened conceptions of life (namely, the *homo laborans* and *homo superstes* concepts) must be considered for the sake of democracy itself. Indeed, these two by-products of biopolitics not only weaken civicism and the sense of people sharing common bounds but also erode freedom by creating an impoverished conception of life that not only makes it tremendously easy to control individuals' actions but also opens the door to a vertical relationship between the state and its citizens in a way that can lead to a form of paternalism that can prove detrimental to people's freedom.

At the end of the day, when circumstances allow for biopolitics to take over as the prevailing form of governance, the presence or absence of the rule of law as a way to distinguish between authoritarian and liberal states (which is usually how these two types of regimes are differentiated from one another) becomes a pretty weak manner of understanding the uniqueness of liberal democracy. What the COVID-19 pandemic has proved (with the war on terror being a precursor in this regard) is that the presence of the rule of law does not prevent the implementation of liberticidal measures that are disproportionate in light of the threat societies are facing and, as a consequence of their extremity, effectively erase the boundaries between freedom and undue restrictions on what people can and cannot do. Paradoxically, this erosion of freedom that we are currently witnessing in liberal democracies is directly linked with the victory of the liberalist ideology over communism some 30 years ago. Nobody thought, at the time (and many still do not see it today), that the 'end of history' would open the door to a new way of thinking about liberalism that would make it easier to banalise unnecessary restrictions on people's freedom in a way that has led liberalism to, slowly but surely, move away from that which it ought to stand. In light of what promises to become the new existential threat humans will have to face (e.g. the climate crisis), saying that the *homo superstes* trend that has resulted from the post-1991 understanding of liberalism might end up aggravating the evolution liberal societies have experienced over the last 30 years is worrying to say the least.

Notes

1 A survey in Saskatchewan, Canada, revealed that almost a third of respondents had reduced contact with relatives because of COVID-19 policy-related disagreements. www.cbc.ca/news/canada/saskatchewan/relationships-Covid-19-saskatchewan-1.6347569
2 More than half of Americans (56%) indicated that they would welcome such regulation. https://morningconsult.com/2021/12/15/social-media-regulation-poll-2022/
3 This was the case in 2021 in the Netherlands and Italy, among other countries.
4 Sustaining people's activities would, of course, require the implementation of certain policies that would allow individuals to meet their primary and basic needs. We can think, in this regard, about a universal basic income financed through a 'robot tax' on companies directly driving job automation. These sorts of proposals have been welcomed in the past by well-known entrepreneurs whose fortune is directly connected with contemporary technologies, such as Elon Musk, Mark Zuckerberg, Bill Gates, and Mark Cuban.

References

Adam, D. (2020). "Special Report: The Simulations Driving the World's Response to COVID-19", *Nature*. April 2 (corrected April 3). www.nature.com/articles/d41586-020-01003-6
Agamben, G. (1998). *Homo Sacer: Sovereign Power and Bare Life*. Stanford: Stanford University Press.
Arendt, H. (1998). *The Human Condition*. Chicago: University of Chicago Press.
Aristotle (1962). *The Politics*, translated by T.A. Sinclair. London: Penguin.
Aristotle (2000). *Nichomachean Ethics*. Cambridge: Cambridge University Press.
Aristotle (2007). *On Rhetoric*, 2nd edition. Oxford: Oxford University Press.
Arntz, M., Gregory, T. & Zierahan, U. (2016). "The Risk of Automation for Jobs in OECD Countries: A Comparative Analysis", May 14.
Bauman, Z. (2000). *Liquid Modernity*. Cambridge: Polity Press.
Beck, U. (1999). *World Risk Society*. Cambridge: Polity Press.
Berriman, R. & Hawksworth, J. (2017). "Will Robots Steal Our Jobs? The Potential Impact of Automation on the UK and Other Major Economies". PwC, March.
Brooks, D. (2014). "The Quality of Fear", *New York Times*, October 20. www.nytimes.com/2014/10/21/opinion/david-brooks-what-the-ebola-crisis-reveals-about-culture.html
Brooks, D. (2019). "An Era Defined by Fear", *New York Times*, April 29. www.nytimes.com/2019/04/29/opinion/politics-fear.html
Burke, G., Federman, J., Wu, H., Pathi, K. & McGuirk, R. (2022). "Police Seize on Covid-19 Tech to Expand Global Surveillance", *Associated Press*. December 21. https://apnews.com/article/technology-police-government-surveillance-Covid-19-3f3f348d176bc7152a8cb2dbab2e4cc4
Caron, J-F. (2019a). *The Prince 2.0: Applying Machiavellian Strategy to Contemporary Political Life*. Singapore: Springer.

References 105

Caron, J-F. (2019b). *Contemporary Technologies and the Morality of Warfare: The War of the Machines*. London: Routledge.
Caron, J-F. (2020). *A Sketch of the World After the Covid-19 Crisis: Essays on Political Authority, the Future of Globalization and the Rise of China*. London: Palgrave MacMillan.
Caron, J-F. (2021a). *Violent Alternatives to War: Justifying Actions Against Contemporary Terrorism*. Berlin: De Gruyter.
Caron, J-F. (2021b). *Irresponsible Citizenship: The Cultural Roots of the Crisis of Authority in Times of Pandemic*. New York: Peter Lang.
Caron, J-F. (2022a). *The Great Lockdown: Western Societies and the Fear of Death*. New York: Peter Lang.
Caron, J-F. (2022b). "Conceptualizing Shame", in Hélène Thibault & Jean-François Caron (eds.), *Uyat or the Culture of Shame in Central Asia*. Singapore: Springer, pp. 15–22.
Caron, J-F. (2022c). *Marginalisé. Réflexions sur l'isolement du Canada dans les relations internationales*. Québec: Presses de l'Université Laval.
Caron, J-F. (2023). *The Moral Dilemmas of Fighting Terrorism and Guerrilla Groups*. Berlin: De Gruyter.
Caron, J-F. & Thibault, H. (2022). *Central Asia and the Covid-19 Pandemic*. Singapore: Springer.
Constant, B. (1988). *Constant: Political Writings*. Translated and edited by Biancamaria Fontana. Cambridge: Cambridge University Press.
"Covid-19: les hospitalisations en pédopsychiatrie ont explosé de 80%". France Info. www.francetvinfo.fr/sante/enfant-ado/Covid-19-les-hospitalisations-en-pedopsychiatrie-ont-explose-de-80_4344365.html
de Tocqueville, A. (2000). *Democracy in America*. Chicago: The University of Chicago Press.
De Wilde, M. (2012). "The dictator's trust: Regulating and constraining emergency powers in the Roman Republic", *History of Political Thought,* Vol. 33, No. 4, pp. 555–577.
Di Stasio, A., Greco, A., de Vincentiis, M. & Ralli, M. (2020). "Mortality rate and gender differences in Covid-19 patients dying in Italy: A comparison with other countries", *European Review for Medical and Pharmacological Sciences,* Vol. 24, pp. 4066–4067.
Dodsworth, L. (2021). *A State of Fear*. London: Pinter & Martin Ltd.
Ebhardt, T., Remondini, C. & Bertacche, M. (2020). "99% of Those Who Died From Virus Had Other Illness, Italy Says", *Bloomberg,* March 18. www.bloomberg.com/news/articles/2020-03-18/99-of-those-who-died-from-virus-had-other-illness-italy-says#xj4y7vzkg
Ferejohn, J. & Pasquino, P. (2004). "The law of exception: A typology of emergency powers", *International Journal of Constitutional Law*, Vol. 2, No. 2, pp. 210–239.

Fletcher, J.F., Bastedo, H. & Hove, J. (2009). "Losing heart: Declining support and the political marketing of the Afghan mission", *Canadian Journal of Political Science*, Vol. 42, No. 4, pp. 911–937.
Foa, R.S. & Mounk, Y. (2016). "The democratic disconnect", *Journal of Democracy*, Vol. 27, No. 3, pp. 5–17.
Ford, M. (2015). *The Rise of Robots: Technology and the Threat of Mass Unemployment*. London: Oneworld.
Foucault, M. (2004). *Sécurité, Territoire, Population. Cours au Collège de France, 1977–1978*. Paris: Gallimard.
Fraser Institute. (2023). "Lockdown: A Final Assessment", January 19. www.fraserinstitute.org/studies/lockdown-a-final-assessment
Frey, C.B. & Osborne, M.A. (2013). "The Future of Employment: How Susceptible Are Jobs to Automation". Oxford Martin Programme on Technology and Employment, September 17. www.oxfordmartin.ox.ac.uk/downloads/academic/The_Future_of_Employment.pdf
Friedrich, C. (1937). *Constitutional Government and Politics: Nature and Development*. New York & London: Harper & Brothers.
Furlong, A. (2021). "Trust Deficit Stalls Vaccinations in Eastern Europe, Driving New COVID Surge", *Politico*, November 8. www.politico.eu/article/Covid-vaccination-eastern-europe-trust-fourth-wave-vaccine/
Garlan, Y. (1974). *Recherches de poliorcétique grecque*. Athens: École française d'Athènes.
Hamilton, A., Madison, J. & Jay, J. (2009). *The Federalist Papers*. New York: Palgrave MacMillan.
Hartz, L. (1955). *The Liberal Tradition in America*. New York: Harcourt, Brace, Jovanovich.
Havel, V. (1986). "Letter to Dr. Gustav Husak", in Jan Vladislav (ed.), *Vaclav Havel: Living in Truth*. London & Boston: Faber and Faber, pp. 3–35.
Hobbes, T. (1994). *Leviathan*. Indianapolis & Cambridge: Hackett.
Hoffmann, C. & Wolf, E. (2021). "Older age groups and country-specific case fatality rates of COVID-19 in Europe, USA and Canada", *Infection: A Journal of Infectious Diseases*, Vol. 49, No. 1, pp. 111–116.
Horowitz, J. & Bubola, E. (2020) "On Day 1 of Lockdown, Italian Officials Urge Citizens to Abide by Rules", *New York Times*, 8 March. www.nytimes.com/2020/03/08/world/europe/italy-coronavirus-quarantine.html
Ikenberry, G.J. (2020). *A World Safe for Democracy: Liberal Internationalism and the Crises of Global Order*. New Haven & London: Yale University Press.
Kahn, P.W. (2002). "The paradox of riskless warfare", *Philosophy and Public Policy*, Vol. 22, No. 3, pp. 2–8.
Kalyvas, A. & Katznelson, I. (2008). *Liberal Beginnings*. New York: Cambridge University Press.

References 107

Kelly, J. (2021). "The Covid-19 Pandemic Caused a Long-Term Joblessness Crisis", *Forbes,* July 10.
Klausser, N. (2022). "État d'urgence et état de droit en France: aspects juridiques. Vers un déséquilibre généralisé des pouvoirs", in Marie Goupy & Yann Rivière (eds.), *De la dictature à l'état d'exception. Approche historique et philosophique.* Rome: École française de Rome, pp. 211–221.
Krishnamurti. (1995). *On Fear.* New York: Harper Collins.
Lee, K.F. (2018). *AI Super-Powers: China, Silicon Valley, and the New World Order.* Houghton Mifflin Harcourt: Boston & New York.
Locke, J. (2003). *Two Treatises of Government and a Letter Concerning Toleration.* New Haven & London: Yale University Press.
Loraux, N. (1986). *The Invention of Athens: The Funeral Oration in the Classical City.* Cambridge, MA: Harvard University Press.
Lubell, N. (2015). "The Problem of Imminence in an Uncertain World", in Marc Weller, Jake William Rylatt & Alexia Solomou (eds.), *The Oxford Handbook of the Use of Force in International Law.* Oxford: Oxford University Press, pp. 697–719.
McBain, S. (2020). "How Covid Is Breaking Up Friendships", *New Statesmen,* December 9. www.newstatesman.com/science-tech/2020/12/how-Covid-19-is-breaking-up-friendships
Mill, J.S. (2001). *On Liberty.* New Haven & London: Yale University Press.
Minnai, F., De Bellis, G., Dragani, T.A. & Colombo, F. (2022). "Covid-19 mortality in Italy varies by patient age, sex and pandemic wave", *Nature,* Vol. 12, p. 4604.
Mitterrand, F. (1964). *Le coup d'état permanent.* Paris: Plon.
Moss, D.M. (2014). "Repression, response, and contained escalation under 'liberalized' authoritarianism in Jordan", *Mobilization,* Vol. 19, No. 3, pp. 261–286.
Mouffe, C. (1994). *La politique et ses enjeux.* Paris: La Découverte.
Palmieri, L., Venacore, N., Donfrancesco, C., Lo Noce, C., Canevelli, M., Punzo, O., Raparelli, V., Pezzotti, P., Riccardo, F., Bella, A., Fabiani, M., Paolo D'Ancona, F., Vaianelle, L., Tiple, D., Colaizzo, E., Palmer, K., Rezza, G., Piccioli, A., Brusaferro, S. & Onder, G. (2020). "Clinical characteristics of hospitalized individuals dying with Covid-19 by age group in Italy", *The Journal of Gerontology,* Vol. 75, No. 9, pp. 1796–1800.
PBS (1992). "Nixon: The American Experience," September 24.
RTBF (2020). March 25. "Coronavirus: 44% des jeunes de 18 à 21 ans ne respecteraient pas les mesures de confinement," www.rtbf.be/info/societe/detail_coronavirus-le-confinement-une-tannee-chez-44-des-jeunes-de-18-a-21-ans-selon-test-achat?id=10467310
Santomauro, D.F. et al. (2021). "Global prevalence and burden of depressive and anxiety disorders in 204 countries and territories in 2020 due to the Covid-19 pandemic", *Lancet,* Vol. 398, pp. 1700–1712.

Schmitt, C. (2014). *Dictatorship*. London: Polity.
Skhlar, J. (1989). "The Liberalism of Fear", in Nancy Rosenblum (ed.), *Liberalism and the Moral Life*. Cambridge: Harvard University Press, pp. 21–38.
Solzhenitsyn, A. (1979). *A World Split Apart: Commencement Address Delivered at Harvard University June 8, 1978*. New York: Harper & Row.
Solzhenitsyn, A. (1980). *L'erreur de l'Occident*. Paris: Grasset.
Sud-Ouest (2020). "Coronavirus: plus de 225 000 verbalisations pour non-respect du confinement", March 26. www.sudouest.fr/2020/03/26/coronavirus-plus-de-225-000-verbalisations-pour-non-respect-du-confinement-7366241-10861.php
Susskind, J. (2018). *Future Politics*. Oxford: Oxford University Press.
Taylor, C. (1992). "Multiculturalism and "The politics of recognition"", in Amy Gutmann (ed.), *The Politics of Recognition*. Princeton, NJ: Princeton University Press, pp. 25–73.
Thénault, S. (2007). "L'état d'urgence (1955–2005): De l'Algérie coloniale à la France métropolitaine: destin d'une loi", *Le mouvement social*, Vol. 1, No. 218, pp. 63–78.
Thucydides (1974). *History of the Peloponnesian War*. London: Penguin.
Usta, J., Murr, H. & El-Jarrah, R. (2021). "Covid-19 lockdown and the increased violence against women: Understanding domestic violence during a pandemic", *Violence & Gender*, Vol. 8, No. 2, pp. 133–139.
Van Noorden, R. (2022). "Covid Death Tolls: Scientists Acknowledge Errors in WHO Estimates", *Nature*, June 1. www.nature.com/articles/d41586-022-01526-0
Walker, S. (1998). *The Rights Revolution: Rights and Community in Modern America*. New York: Oxford University Press.
Wallerstein, I. (2003). "Citizens all? Citizens Sime! The making of the citizen", *Comparative Studies in Society and History*, Vol. 45, No. 4, pp. 650–679.
Walzer, M. (1985). *Exodus and Revolution*. New York: Basic Books.
Walzer, M. (2006). *Just and Unjust Wars: A Moral Argument with Historical Illustrations*, 4th edition. New York: Basic Books.
Watkins, F.M. (1940). "The problem of constitutional dictatorship", *Public Policy*, Vol. 1, pp. 324–379.
Wenner Moyer, M. (2022). "The Covid generation: How is the pandemic affecting kids' brains", *Nature*, January 12. www.nature.com/articles/d41586-022-00027-4
Wright, T.J. (2017). *All Measures Short of War: The Contest for the 21st Century & the Future of American Power*. New Haven & London: Yale University Press.

Index

Agamben, Giorgio 20
agonism 1, 83
Al Qaeda 54
Arendt, Hannah 20–1, 23, 26, 45
Aristotle 20–1, 45, 51
authoritarian 1–5, 7–9, 28, 59, 63, 71–2, 78, 86, 90–1, 94

biological life 21–3, 38, 51, 98–9, 101
biopolitics 1, 19, 29, 97–9, 102; *see also* biological life

climate change 40–1, 54, 61, 63
cold war 1, 19–20, 33, 35–9, 43, 47, 50, 55, 58, 61–2, 64, 82, 92–4, 98
Constant, Benjamin 50
communism 2, 8, 20, 32, 36, 38, 43, 45, 48, 50, 58, 61–2, 75, 103

De Gaulle, Charles 70–1, 78, 82, 87
De Tocqueville, Alexis 5–6, 15, 50, 92
democracy 1, 27, 46, 49, 59, 65, 69–71, 77–8, 85–6, 91, 102
dictatorship 45, 61, 68, 70–1, 75, 85, 87–8

enlightenment 19, 24, 28–31, 38

Foucault, Michel 2, 20, 53
Fukuyama, Francis 32

Havel, Vaclav 4–6, 8–9, 61
Hobbes, Thomas 14, 47–52, 54, 57–8, 65–6; *see also* Hobbesian
Hobbesian 47, 51–61, 63, 81, 83, 93, 100–1
homo laborans 21, 97, 102
homo superstes 19, 29, 31–2, 36, 40, 43, 58, 62, 68, 75, 78–82, 84–5, 91–4, 98–9, 102–3

liberalism of fear 34–6, 38–9, 47–8, 63, 72, 98–9
liberticidal 1, 9, 13–14, 18–19, 29, 32, 43, 47, 55–7, 62–3, 72, 74, 84, 93–4, 100, 102
life-threatening 13, 39–41, 68, 77–8, 83–4, 93
Locke, John 48–9, 51–2, 54, 59, 65, 68, 70
Lockean 14, 47–8, 51–3, 58–9, 61–3, 72, 78, 81, 83, 91–4, 98, 100–1; *see also* Lockean

Macron, Emmanuel 12, 80
Mill, John Stuart 5–6, 15

9/11 38, 54, 59, 72, 74, 83

Oikos 21, 26, 29, 99

Patriot Act 59, 74
Pericles 22, 33, 51
polis 21, 23

post heroic 30, 41, 43–4, 97
private sphere 5, 21, 23, 28
public sphere 21–3, 26–9, 45, 47,
    82–4, 97–9

Skhlar, Judith 34, 48, 65
Solzhenitsyn, Alexander 31, 45

state of emergency 13, 64, 71–2,
    75, 78–80, 84, 87–8

terrorism 38, 59, 73–6, 80
Trudeau, Justin 80–1
tyranny 6–7, 15, 36, 48, 50, 63,
    90–4, 99